WEST-COUNTRY STORIES

WEST-COUNTRY STORIES

STORIES

BY

A. L. ROWSE

LONDON

MACMILLAN & CO. LTD

1945

COPYRIGHT

PRINTED IN GREAT BRITAIN
BY R. & R. CLARK, LIMITED, EDINBURGH

PREFACE

ONE word about my title. After some hesitation I have decided to call this book " West-Country Stories ". I use the word " stories " in its older sense, going back to the Middle Ages, to include narratives both of fact and fiction. In any case the stories of invention, even though mostly ghost stories, have a foundation of fact ; while the narratives of fact, I hope, are not wholly without imagination. And I call the book " West-Country Stories ", for though nearly the whole of it is concerned with Cornwall, in one or two places I cross the Tamar boundary.

Most of these pieces were written before the war. In re-reading them now it is touching to reflect how the apprehensions expressed in some of them for the visible memorials of our past have been all too bitterly borne out, especially in the cases of Plymouth and Exeter. Perhaps some of these descriptions may serve to bring back things of beauty in the West Country as they were, now gone for ever.

Some of these stories first appeared in *The Times Literary Supplement, Country Life, Nineteenth Century, Listener, Time and Tide, West Briton*, and the *St. Austell Hospital Handbook*, to which I make acknowledgment. " Pageant of Plymouth " is the original draft of the B.B.C. broadcast in honour of the Quincentenary of Plymouth's Charter in 1939. Other pieces are new and appear here for the first time.

A. L. ROWSE

POLMEAR MINE
 ST. AUSTELL
  Autumn 1944

TO DEAR

DR. STEPHENS OF NEWQUAY

SCHOLAR AND ANTIQUARY

IN MEMORY OF

OUR FRIEND

CONTENTS

THE WICKED VICAR OF
LANSILLIAN

IT is well known to the inhabitants of the parish of Lansillian that they have a ghost to their credit — or to their discredit, as they seem to think. For they won't tell you about him — they won't own up to him, until you have gone a long way in their intimacy. Not an easy thing, as anybody who knows Cornish people can vouch.

I was once present when an antiquarian friend of mine tried to draw a farmer of that parish on the subject. No one more patient or pertinacious. But the farmer was wonderfully evasive. He knew the story all right. But he wasn't going to tell it — certainly not to a stranger. Everybody in the parish knew the story. It would be interesting to go into the reasons why they would not tell it : parish pride, the fear of ridicule, superstitious fear disguised as a propitiatory incredulity, or a simple taboo ?

But the fact is that in the eighteenth century the parish of Lansillian had a very wicked vicar. He was called Cowell. He was not a Cornishman : he came from over the border somewhere, nobody quite knew where : some people said from " op Lunnon way " — from which, of course, you might expect anything. His doings in his lifetime were so dark and questionable that after his death he had little rest, and gave the parish no more peace than he had while he was alive. He haunted the place, so that his ghost had to be laid. Which it was : his evil spirit took refuge in a black cockerel, which, after an exciting chase all over the parish, was at length shut up in a cloam-oven. (You know, of course, what a cloam-oven is ? — one of those old-fashioned earthenware ovens built in at the side of an open fire. Old people in Cornwall used to say that no bread was like that baked in a cloam-oven.) A few elderly people in the parish of Lansillian know the place where the black cock was shut up. But they wouldn't tell you for worlds.

So far everybody knows. The rest is known to few. I am going to tell it you. With the aid of a little research in the parish registers, among the wills of the Archdeacon's Probate Court, and the marriage licences of the Vicar-General of the diocese, I have been able to piece together the main outlines of the story. It is inevitable that there should be some imputation of motive, but not, I hope, more than may warrantably be inferred from the facts recovered.

Lansillian is a moorland parish with a particular character of its own : its air has that mixture of sharpness and sweetness which goes to the head like wine. There the gorse is more golden in spring, the heather more purple, and the bracken a richer russet in winter, than anywhere else. The scents are keener, purer ; the tang of camomile on the moor, and that lovely lime-like scent of young bracken shoots. The parish is full of rocks and stones ; but its character is chiefly given by the beautiful, deep, winding valley which runs through it, with its boulders and remnants of glacial moraines — a paradise of wild vegetation.

Even today there is only one bus a week that reaches it ; in Georgian days it was, of course, infinitely remote.

In those days — the last years of the reign of George I and the first of George II — the living was held by the Reverend Nathaniel Tregenza, in his bachelor days Fellow of Exeter College, Oxford. An offshoot of a respectable old Cornish family, connected with other still better-to-do families with livings in their gift, he had made a success of life. He was, at the age of sixty-six, a benevolent pluralist of a rich vintage. Nor had he less success in the more dubious exchange of matrimony. His

2

first wife was an heiress in a small way : she brought him
a useful property in the shape of ground-rents and houses
in the neighbouring town of Bodmin. At the mature age
of sixty-four he could well afford to marry for fancy —
and the parish was surprised, not to say somewhat
scandalised, by the appearance of a magnificent, red-
headed young beauty to share the comforts of the fine
new vicarage he had built for himself.

Never addicted in an unhealthy way to the performance of unnecessary duties (the old man adhered to the
motto of *Quieta non movere* so dear to the heart of the
Minister—with whom, for the rest, he was much in agree-
ment), the vicar, on his second marriage, had handed
over the cares of the neighbouring parish, the rectory of
which he also held, to an active-bodied curate : the
Reverend Mark Cowell. As we shall see, he was no less
active of mind than of body. We may wonder why it was
that a person of such ability and determination had got
no further, when already in early middle age, than a mere
curacy in a remote Cornish parish. The answer, I fear,
is not far to seek : he was a person of low birth, and there
was a certain coarseness of manner which betrayed his
origin and did not recommend him in that snobbish age.

But he was ingratiating ; and once having found a
foothold with the Tregenzas, he was determined to make
the most of it. His very origin, and retarded success in
the world, spurred him on in the course which left such a
curious mark upon the parish. To the old man he was
infinitely obliging — and even more useful. It must be
admitted that the faculties of the rubicund old vicar were
in a decline, aided by frequent potations of port. The
Reverend Mr. Cowell not only did duty in the parish of
which he was curate, but he formed the habit of coming
over to take duty for the vicar in Lansillian itself. And
what was more, his services were unremunerated — or
they were for the present. Tregenza, though a jovial, had

3

always been a *careful*, man ; by this time he was worth
a solid, handsome fortune, and there was no one else to
leave it to but his honey-pot young wife.

The curate's pressing attentions at the vicarage were
not without a further inducement. He found favour in
the young woman's eye. Nor was his elevation in her
affections due entirely to the flatness of the surrounding
country. It cannot be denied that he was a fine figure of
a man ; upstanding, with the aggressive virility of some
male animal ; very dark in a saturnine way, with glossy
black hair which rose to an assertive crest on the top of
his head — he could never habituate himself to a wig ;
marked, salient features which gave him a look corvine,
indeed, rather than aquiline ; round, black eyes that
looked at you boldly, fiercely, then suddenly blinked.

What more natural than that such a prepossessing
figure should engage the unattached affections of a
vigorous but uncherished spouse ? Or that he should
think of the future in terms of the eligible fortune that
would be hers when the old man died ? The vicar's
powers were flagging ; but they might go on flagging for
a good many years yet. There is no doubt that his
decline into the grave was aided from an extraneous
source. At least the parish had no doubt of it.

As to what happened in the vicarage of Lansillian on
Christmas Day 1743 we know only this.

The curate had ridden over the frost-bound moorland
tracks that morning to take service there. The vicar and
his lady had bidden him to their Christmas dinner, which
in these remote parts was as early as noon. After the
lady had left table, the two clergymen remained long
into the afternoon doing justice, and rather more than
justice, to the vicar's port. And it was the vicar himself
who chiefly played the part of judge.

The thin, wavering light was beginning to fail among
the stripped beeches ; already an early owl was hooting

4

in the Valley across from the glebe. In the lowlands of Cornwall this was a green Christmas. But in these uplands the rime made a myriad lovely patterns upon branch and twig, upon the anatomies of the trees, the spires of the grass. It was — and is — a cold parish ; but that afternoon the fire leaped cheerfully in the dining-room of the vicarage with its plain, unpainted panelling of pine.

The port was finished. The vicar insisted upon fetching up another bottle. This meant a journey down to the capacious cellar of which he was proud, and which he liked showing off to his guests. The curate did not deny him, though he offered to take the keys and perform the commission for him. That settled the resolution of the vicar to go himself. Rising a little unsteadily to his legs, he took the arm of his faithful companion. They left the room together. The old man never left the cellar alive.

Of course it was very easy to account for his death. The house fell away on that side of the hill, and the cellar was deep and dark, with a long steep flight of stone steps into it. On one side the steps had a wall for support ; on the other there was as yet no hand-rail : it had not been finished. It was very easy to miss your footing on those steps ; it was easy to trip up — or to be tripped up, if you were an old feeble man, with a fortune to leave to a young wife, and that wife had given you pledges of her favour.

Or so the parish said. Cowell roundly declared that the vicar had had too much to drink and accused himself of insufficient care in looking after him. He deposed that while he was on the threshold attending to the rushlight which threatened to go out, the vicar had fallen from top to bottom of the steps and broken his neck — while he himself hardly knew what was happening. Nothing improbable in that. The vicar had certainly broken his neck. There was only one little discrepancy : there was no decipherable mark upon those new stone steps down

5

which the vicar's unwieldy body was presumed to have fallen.

Not that there was anything conclusive in that either. It was merely that the parish knew — in the obscure, subterraneous way in which the parish gets to know everything — that the vicar's body had not fallen to the foot of the steps at all, but over the edge, where there was no hand-rail. Only a slight impulse, a gentle persuasive propulsion would be enough — and the parish was convinced that that propulsion had been given. But there was no proving anything ; and perhaps guilt would not have so universally affixed itself to the person of the curate if it had not been for the subsequent course of events.

First, he married the widow, and in a scandalously short time after the — well, shall I say, mishap ? That I have verified from the parish register, where the entry stands :

March ye 1st The Revd Mark Cowell, Clerk in Holy Orders, this day md Mrs Mary Tregenza, widow of the Revd Nathaniel Tregenza, late Vicar of this parish.

By license.

Second, he succeeded not only to the vicar's widow with her desirable portion, but also to his vicarage, and that within a matter of months.

On that subject the rumour in the parish was quite definite and apparently well-informed : it was that to his other misdeeds he had added the sin of simony — that he had purchased the presentation from a venal, if uninstructed, patron.

Even so the conviction against him in the neighbourhood might have become mollified if his later course of conduct had been conformable. But it was not. He terrorised his young wife : he exercised a malign and brutal ascendancy over her ; in a few years she pined away and died. He was already in possession of her property, and he proved himself a merciless oppressor of the poor. Never a charitable act was known of him in all the twenty years he continued as vicar. He ended as a sordid miser: the insecurity of his beginnings compensating itself in his later life.

Yet in his way he had been successful. He had got where he meant to be. He did not seem to mind that he was a shunned and hated man. Like Machiavelli's Prince he thought it better to be feared. So it may be seen that not always in life is evil rewarded according to its deserts.

But in after-life?

Well, it was here that he found retribution. His spirit could not rest. Like Tregeagle, the unjust steward, before him, his ghost roamed the countryside. The neighbourhood could not rest for him. Sometimes people saw him riding his black nag across the moorland between Lansillian and the next parish. More often he was seen haunting the corner of the churchyard where his predecessor and patron lay buried. Most frequently of all, he was to be seen along the vicarage drive, usually at the curve looking to the house, especially by moonlight or in the twilight.

Something had to be done about it. The place was tormented by his evil shade. What more natural than that the people should ask his successor to lay the ghost? He was indeed very willing.

A few persons in the parish had thought of calling in the assistance of the holy Mr. Wesley, then on his first evangelising tours of the county. He was known to entertain strong and orthodox views on the subject of ghosts — had he not suffered in youth, along with all his family, from the persecutions of " Jeremy " ? He had already a small following in the parish ; but in the end conservatism prevailed over curiosity. The greater number doubted the efficacy of his ministrations ; the rest

7

couldn't wait for his next visit. They turned the more readily to their own pastor, who himself had an interest in the matter.

It was arranged that the laying of the ghost should take place at daybreak — when ghosts return to their graves — in the churchyard. The new vicar, though young, was a scholar, and not a word did he say to the ghost in English. What he had to say he said in Latin, reading from a book and making the sign of the Cross. "In nomine Patris et Filii et Spiritus Sancti", he began bravely. The parishioners stood round in a crowd, straddling over the graves and giving each other the courage of proximity. Some of them were armed with sticks and staves, others with flails and hooks. It was a cold, windy, Easter morning ; the teeth of some of the gathering chattered in their mouths. They were all strung-up. At the unaccustomed words, that had been uttered so often before on that spot in bygone ages, some obscure, atavistic impulse stirred in the crowd and made them all one. At the words "in nomine Domini", uttered three times by the parson, one old woman of immense age mumbled after him "nummy-dummy" and crossed herself devoutly : she had been brought up as a child at St. Mawgan, where the Catholic Arundells still lived, and at this solemn, scarecrow hour her mind went back instinctively to her Catholic childhood. She seemed for a passing moment the voice of the people and their age-long past : the scene shifted back to the Middle Ages, the priest and the people taking part in antiphony in some dimly-remembered pre-Reformation rite.

Then at the words " Retro me, Sathanas " there was a sudden screech among the bushes and a great shining black cock flew high into the air.

The people knew exactly what it was.

" God bless my soul if 'tedn the very image of passon Cow'll," said a farmer standing near by the apparition.

The great ominous bird soared right over the church-yard wall, and half running, half flying, made down the little street of the church town for the Valley.

"After'n," cried a hundred voices with one accord. There started such a hue and cry as had not been heard since the Gadarene swine rushed down a steep place into the sea. The whole parish thrilled with excitement; the dogs joined in, barking like mad; pigs screamed, ponies whinnied ; men, women, and boys ran shouting down the street, the splendid saturnine bird with his great crest before them. Some obscure impulse led the creature, at once terrified and terrifying, to follow the bounds of the parish. Across the Valley he leaped and flew to Boswerra — all the cattle were disturbed and frightened ; from Boswerra farm to Bosloggett ; from Bosloggett to the toll-gate on the turnpike road, the crowd following, aiming sticks and stones, but not yet catching up. Thence he flew across the bit of moorland to Trenaddern ; from Trenaddern to the quarry, where it seemed he was fairly cornered.

The bird — or whatever creature it was — was be-ginning to flag ; some of its feathers had been torn by well-timed blows, but the devilish look in its eye was as fierce and unyielding as ever. The crowd closed in : "The gashly varmint," a voice shouted ; "Kill'n," rose the cry all round. The mouth of the quarry was now closed : a panting mob with sticks and staves held it. Yet they were still foiled : with one last effort the creature, talons and wings full extended, scaled the great boulder that blocked the side and made once more, by a fatal impulse, back to the church town. As it struggled up the steep narrow street, granite cottages on either side, almost back to its starting point, the crowd gained upon it. Battered, exhausted, the creature made for an open door. "We've got'n," yelled the crowd, bursting in.

Nothing in the bare kitchen at all but a cloam-oven.

The leaders drew their own conclusion. They weren't going to put hand or head inside that oven, for all that their blood was up. In a trice the door was closed upon whatever it was that was inside, the peat and faggots piled up against the door. And later in the day the oven was sealed up for good and all.

THE STONE THAT LIKED
COMPANY

IT was the Christmas vacation : and those few Fellows who were still up — happy to see the backs of their undergraduates and to be quit of the dreary routine of lectures and tutorials for a blessed five weeks — had fore-gathered that evening, after a quiet common-room dinner, in the rooms of the Dean. The Dean, in spite of his name, was a secular, a very secular person ; his inclinations were hospitable, indeed he was rather overmuch given to entertaining. Though he had the cold, wary eyes of an intelligent fish, he was in fact a jovial person, not happy unless he had one or two of his friends in after dinner to sip his admirable port.

Tonight they were five : four of them drinking port and one — the wisest of them — with his glass of bur-gundy. This last was just raising his glass to his lips, when suddenly the lights went out. In itself no remarkable, nor that winter infrequent, circumstance ; for it had happened several times of late that there had been a breakdown at the electric light works from which the college current came. The winter was a severe one ; floods had broken out by the river and the works flooded. There was no knowing how long before the light would come on again.

Patient men, sitting heavy after a substantial meal, they sat there for a moment, their faces lit up momentarily by the gleams from the oak-log burning in the grate. Then the Dean rose, fetched out of the corner cupboard two pleasant little candlesticks, lit them and placed them on the mantelpiece : their flame, when it caught up, revealed their pretty Regency pattern, a single column with a wreath of foliage running round the stem.

"Hadn't somebody better tell a story?" said the Economics don : a hearty man with rubicund face and white sweater to match. He had a knack of saying what everybody thought.

"Yes, let's tell sad stories of the death of kings," said the English don, a young man who had only recently joined the college.

"Well, who's got a story to tell?" said the Dean.

The general opinion was that he had ; indeed he was well known for his stories. As host he couldn't very well have declined, even if he had wanted to. It was a situation he loved, for his inclination was all in favour of a story — his own story, and himself telling it.

"Well, since you will have it——" he began, settling himself well into the back of his chair, his head between the two side flaps in deep shadow, looking more than ever like some queer extinct animal with large flapping ears, while from the depths gleamed those intelligent eyes behind the spectacles. "There's a house in Cornwall that I know——" he went on.

"Oh ! come, Mr. Dean," said the Economics don, who knew well the Dean's penchant for old houses in Cornwall haunted by ghosts.

"Well, as a matter of fact, it's not that kind of house at all," said the Dean, quite unperturbed. "It's a modern house, built after the last war. In fact, it's a bungalow, or what I believe is called a semi-bungalow. Some friends of mine took it for a bit some years ago, perhaps as much as fifteen years ago — how time flies ! *Pereunt et impu-tantur.* They took it for a bit. They didn't stay there long." He paused, dug further into the back of his chair, hugging himself, then resumed.

"I said ' friends of mine ' : but really it was the widow of a friend of mine and her son, a delicate lad, liable to asthma and bronchitis, and that sort of thing. He was very highly strung, I gather, but intelligent and extremely sensitive — at any rate, he was as a child, the only time that I saw him. The mother took this house in Cornwall for the benefit of his health because of the climate. The climate agreed with him ; it wasn't the climate that——"

" What was it ? " said the eager young English lecturer, not used to the Dean's roundabout way of telling a story.

" Just you wait, young man," said he, not at all put out. " The house was ideal from their point of view : not too large, very convenient, and could be run with one servant and a man in occasionally to look after the garden. My friend, Mrs. Wilford, took a great deal of interest in it. Not so the boy : perhaps it would have been better for him if he had.

" His hobby was antiquities. He was just about the age when boys are mad about archæology, would go chasing off on his bicycle to take rubbings of brasses in Cornish churches and all that sort of thing. Probably did him no good : he was a restless, inquiring sort of lad who could never take things easily. There was always an element of overstrain about him. I suppose he must have been eighteen or nineteen : he would have been up here if it hadn't been for his health. I'm not sure that he wasn't a good deal spoiled by his mother : her only child, and he being rather an invalid. He was good-looking, too, like his father : I saw a photograph of him after — well, after what happened. He had that striking combination of jet-black hair with deep-blue eyes which you sometimes come across in Scots people. He was tall and rather overgrown. There was a curious fanatic look in his eyes. He had another passion, too, besides archæology — music. He would sit for hours listening to concerts on the wireless — in those early days of wireless. He was beginning to compose, too : not very professional, perhaps, but he certainly had a streak of something, more than talent.

" It so happened that a couple of fields away from

the house there was a longstone : one of those megaliths which you get in Cornwall and Ireland — this was a particularly fine specimen.   The Devil's Walking-stick, the local people called it : they have some story about how it came to be there — you know the kind of thing. It is there no longer.   After what happened——"

There was a movement of impatience on the part of the eager young man.   The Dean poured himself out a second glass of burgundy in leisurely fashion.

"Well — some of the young miners thereabouts got together one night and blew it up."

"What ? " said the Classics don in a tone of horror : he was himself interested in archæology in a mild way. "An interesting megalithic monument like that, destroyed by these vandals only a few years ago ?   I've never heard of such a thing.   How did it come to happen ?   Of course, we all know that in previous centuries when people didn't value these things, didn't know what they were, they sometimes broke them up and used them for gate-posts on their farms, or for road-stone."

"How do you know that they didn't know what they were doing ? " said the Dean, with an odd tone in his voice.   His eyes had a curious intense look in them. "That they meant to break it up, and did it deliber- ately ?   They might have been *afraid*" — he underlined the word significantly with his smooth voice — " and even though they were afraid, they nevertheless went through with it.   I call that courage of a sort.

"You wouldn't have heard of it," he resumed in his ordinary speaking voice, with no suggestion in it.   "No- thing was said about it in public.   All the local people were in it : they knew who had done it all right.   But they never would say ; for they all wanted it done.   And I think," he said, fixing the Classics don with his eyes, " after you have heard what I am going to tell you, you will agree that they were not without reason.

" Of course it was an enormous attraction to the house in young Christopher's eyes when he first discovered the stone. He took it as if he were its first discoverer — ' silent upon a peak in Darien ' and that sort of thing — would he had been, poor lad !

" As a matter of fact, he could get nothing out of the local inhabitants about the stone or its history. They knew nothing about it — or said they knew nothing about it. In itself sufficiently curious when you come to think of it, for it was an exceedingly fine one. Young Christopher himself took its measurements. He found that it was over nine feet above ground : that meant that there must have been at least four or five feet more buried in its socket underground. At its broadest it was about two feet nine inches ; it had a curious shape, for beneath the head the stone was, of course, unhewn ; it had not, so far as one could tell, been shaped by human hands — all the same it gave the impression, a very strong one, of having a head slender and pointed. But beneath the head it broadened out noticeably on one side like a huge mis-shapen shoulder, rather threatening in appearance.

" Christopher was wildly anxious to dig round it, expose the socket if possible, and see what he could find. He never mentioned it to anyone — nobody seemed to be interested. It never occurred to him to ask permission of anyone — least of all of the stone," the Dean added quietly.

" One autumn afternoon — there was nobody about much on that part of the coast — he started operations upon the socket. It was all very enthusiastic and unwise : if he had been successful and got on far enough with it he might have loosened the stone sufficiently for it to have toppled over — perhaps on to him. But he didn't get so far as that. He had no experience of digging or of professional archæology : he was just the enthusiastic amateur. You will agree, my dear Done," he said, addressing the historian among them, who had so far not spoken, was in fact struck by the story, which touched a chord in his experience — " you will agree that there is no more dangerous person — even though the danger is more to himself than to others." The Dean leaned forward, took up his glass from the little mahogany wine-bracket by the fireside, sipped two mouthfuls of burgundy, and went on.

" Young Christopher didn't as a matter of fact get very far with his digging operations. It was a pleasant enough day when he set out across the intervening fields, with their magnificent view of the bay spread out beneath in a kind of shelving curve ; for the stone stands — or rather stood — in a splendid natural situation overlooking the bay. In primitive days before the coppices and plantations thereabouts had been laid out, and when all the fields were open downs, an uncultivated moor, it must have been a dominating object on the skyline from the coast below : a long forefinger pointing heavenwards, perhaps a propitiatory object, no doubt the centre of the religious cult of the primitive people round about, almost certainly the scene of human sacrifice with its attendant rites.

" The boy had not been long at work, heaving up the earth feverishly, in a frantic state of excitement — very bad for him — when there came on, as happens in Cornwall at that time of year, a sudden change in the weather. The sky was quickly filled with lowering grey cloud, which cast a cold uncomfortable atmosphere upon the scene — you know that sinister grey half-light than which there is nothing more cheerless in the world, or more sinking to the spirits. You might have felt a sensation of well-being and contentment a moment before, and then this dark cloud comes down upon you like a weight of lead. From being a warm afternoon it became suddenly cold ; and very soon there followed a stiff shower of hail, for shelter from which Christopher ran to the heavy stone hedge, such as you have in the West Country. While sheltering there he was struck by the changed appearance of the stone. Whether it was that he was cowering down for shelter from the blast, it seemed to him that the stone had grown enormously larger. He noticed how it looked exactly to the west and the setting sun, and the thought of primitive sacrifice came into his mind. He almost fancied that he could see the blood running into the groove that he had exposed, hear the demented shrieks of the gibbering throng in that

> Home of the silent vanuished races,

like the innumerable mammering of bats' voices in the air. There was something horrible in the threatening headlessness of the stone, the shapelessness that was yet suggestive of power, of a ruthless natural force imprisoned in it incapable of expressing itself, or of any release. Suddenly, terrified, he could bear it no longer. But he was a lad of courage and he was too proud to take to his heels. He withdrew in good order, even going so far as to retrieve his pick and shovel, but having the feeling that he was fighting a rear-guard action all the way out of the field and over the hedge. It was the end of his digging operations. He had had a scare — even if it had been possible to resume, which it was not ; for the hail shower was the prelude to a blizzard, which very unwontedly snowed them up for a week or two. It was the stone that resumed operations, in its own way, in its own time."

There was a pause. A coal fell from the fire into the grate. The Dean leaned forward and put another log on, which burned up brightly, lighting up the intent faces of his colleagues. He sank back into the shadows. You could hear the soft ticking of his tiny clock in its Chippendale case, with the little lion's head handles, on the mantelpiece.

" The scare that he had had did not put the boy off. It might have been better if it had. - I repeat that he was a lad of courage, like his father ; though very excitable and nervous, he had spirit. The scare only increased his fascination for the stone : he longed to know more about it, to get to the bottom of it. He was determined to go on — you know the way such boys have of never letting sleeping dogs lie, they won't let a thing alone when it's better it should be — even if that stone had been a sleeping dog and prepared to be left alone.

" During those weeks of snow and sleet and slush " —

(Fire and fleet and candle-lighte
And Christe receive thy saule

— the words ran through the mind of the young English don) — " very exceptional for Cornwall," commented the prosaic mind of the Dean, " Christopher got to work to read everything he could lay hand on that might give him some information. He began naturally with Carew's *Survey of Cornwall* — his father had had a copy of the very pleasant 1769 edition. He drew a blank : nothing whatever about the stone. He went on to all the other old histories of Cornwall, Polwhele, Borlase, Davies Gilbert. Borlase's *Natural Antiquities of Cornwall* did mention the stone and its position, but gave no further particulars.

" However, his reading was not without some effect, for he gathered two bits of information which enabled him to piece together a picture of the district in primitive times in his mind. Less than a mile away, towards the other end of the bay, was a farm called Castle Dennis. There was a stile-field just above the farm, with a path leading across it which cut off a roundabout corner going by the road. After you left the field by the second stile, you found yourself deep in a little lane leading to the third. It was a favourite walk of his. For some reason the field had got the name ' the Field of the Dead ' in his mind. It always had a curious intimate feeling for him : ' Campo dei Morti ' he would say over to himself crossing it, and one day he wrote a poem about it in which occurred the line—

So many dead men have made this their home.

But it had never occurred to him, what now he learned from these old authorities, that that field actually was the inside of a primitive camp, that the little lane into which you descended was the deep ditch or foss outside the rampart ; that the name Castle Dennis was a corruption of the old Celtic *dinas*, meaning fortress. He learned, too, that at the other end of the bay, not far from the longstone, there had been a series of barrows which had been broken into in the eighteenth century and robbed of their funeral urns with their contents of charred human bones.

" The whole picture of the district as it was in primitive times came clear in his mind. There at the other end of the bay had been their encampment, their town, for centuries : there was even a little cliff castle down upon the headland for refuge in time of danger, in those dangerous days when life was so precarious. At the opposite end of the bay was the town of the dead, the cemetery with its barrows where they buried the burned bones of their chieftains. Near the latter was the longstone, the centre of their worship with its fearful barbarous rites.

" In a fever of excitement he read on and on in those weeks. From works on Cornwall he turned to books on stone-age Britain, on the megalithic period, on megalithic religion, on Avebury and Stonehenge. It made a strong, an unforgettable impression when he read that when the altar-stone at Stonehenge was excavated they had found the cleft skull of an infant, evidently a dedicatory sacrifice. He could not forget it. Still his mind raced on and on, forgetting everything else, putting on one side his music, poetry — neglecting everything for the sake of this passion, this morbid fascination.

" At the same time his reading had made him very knowledgeable about the history of the locality. When some local female society — I think it was a Women's Institute — kept badgering his mother to go and lecture to them, his mother, who was a very shy and timid woman, let him go and take her place. He promised he would give them a lecture on the history of their parish — very bold of him, but he had the temperament for it, and what with his enthusiasm and good looks it was a great success. Of course it was all, or mainly, about the longstone and the portrait of the district in primitive times that he had constructed in his mind. He told them that here was one of the finest megalithic monuments in the county — by far the oldest historical monument in the district — and nobody seemed the least proud of its possession or even interested in it. One had never even heard of its existence. Oughtn't it to be put on the map, etc. ? He ended by asking them for any information they had about it, any stories connected with it. The audience did not seem to take the subject up with any enthusiasm ; they were more interested in him. He was too young to note that in fact they rather sheered off it, and quite deftly — though in the manner of Cornish people purely instinctively — they succeeded in deflecting him from it.

" But a day or two later when walking in the vicinity he ran into a woman who stopped him and talked to him about the subject. She was an odd sort of woman, rather masculine in type with a way of swinging to and fro on her hips as if she were a sailor. She was, as a matter of fact, the wife of the captain of a vessel, and prided herself on the fact : so perhaps she got the habit from him. She came close up to the young man, putting her face into his — he stepped down off the pavement unobtrusively into the gutter to give her room.

" ' By the way, Mr. Wilford,' she said, ' you won't know me. My name is Mrs. Chynoweth. But I was very interested by the lecture you gave to our institute the other day. You spoke of the old longstone over there in the field. Well, I remember Mr. Coombe who used to live in the farm just below, and his family before him for a hundred years back ; and he used to say that there was a tradition that somebody had been executed there — oh, hundreds of years ago. I don't mean executed just like that, you know——'

" ' You mean — human sacrifice ? ' said Christopher ; somehow there flashed across his mind what he had read of somewhere, the picture of some poor creature left out on a last outpost of rock facing the setting sun, with a loaf of bread and a pitcher, the tide around those islands rising higher and higher.

" ' Yes, that's it,' she said, rolling her fine dark eyes at him and revealing her powerful dentures in a broad smile. ' And I remember,' she went on, ' when we were children in the village we never used to play in that field. Nobody ever did, or went into it if they could help it.' She moved nearer to him, like an old man of the sea whom he couldn't shake off even if he would ; though he was in fact fascinated. ' Have you ever noticed how threatening it looks with that great heavy shoulder, crouching like somebody ready to lurch out at you ? ' She made the motion expressively with her heavy body. Christopher moved a shade further away. ' Just as if they were waiting to attack you,' she said.

" Christopher did not encourage these suppositions ; they made all the greater impression upon him.

" ' Are you interested in spiritualism ? ' she said, and without waiting for an answer continued, 'Well, I am. And once in London when I went to a spiritualist church and they asked for questions, I thought I'd ask about this old longstone and whether it had any influence upon people's lives round about. The answer came that I was psychic, and should keep away from such things : they are liable to exert a sinister influence on you.'

" Deviating into egoism, released and unashamed, she ceased to be interesting. Christopher found some halting excuse, took his leave, and went on his way.

" His way took him back along the coast by the path that skirted the field where the stone was. From the shelter of the hedge he could observe the figure, as it were without being observed. There was no doubt it bore an extraordinary resemblance to the figure of a hooded and shrouded woman. The great bulging shoulder might be a child it was carrying, that it had taken in its arms for some purpose, draped and veiled. But it was the very formlessness of it, the shaped shapelessness, the fact that headless it seemed to have a head, shoulderless and arm-less it seemed to have shoulders and arms, or at least on this side shoulder and arm ; the blankness of it, standing there through the centuries looking to the west with un-seeing eyes, a blind face to the setting sun, that made it at once so terrible and so pathetic. For tonight he could see its pathos, its loneliness, the embodiment of grey despair, deserted for centuries by its votaries, living its own terrible secret life, the embodiment of imprisoned force.

" Greatly affected by the spectacle and his own teeming imaginings, he hurried by. Yet when he crossed the gap of the gate, from which he could be observed, he could not but feel a distinct tremor run through his nerves. Greatly daring, he turned back for a last look. The stone looked quite different : a bar of angry light from the west rested upon its upper face : it looked blank, im-personal, menacing.

" Christopher had been pestering his mother for days to come and visit the stone with him, wanted to have the name of the house changed to Longstone House, so great was his mania on the subject. At last, not in the least interested, she went along with him to pacify him. That same evening he quarrelled bitterly with her. It was their first (and last) quarrel : they had never so much as bickered before. But that night Christopher, led on by what impulse, uttered things to his mother — about his father, for example, whom he scarcely remembered — such as had never even entered his head before. It was as if a preternaturally old experience of life had suddenly been injected into his veins.

" From that moment everything began to go wrong. As if he had some presentiment of this and of how things would end, he began to keep secretly a journal of the terrible experience that he was to undergo. Later, his mother sent it to me, and after her death it remained in my possession.

" Rarely can a lad of his years have endured such hallucinations — if hallucinations they were that led to such an indubitable result.

" From the eastern windows of the house, where Christopher's bedroom was on the ground floor, the longstone was visible, as I have said, across a couple of intervening fields. It seems that the lad got the sense that he was being ceaselessly watched. One night as he was going to bed late, as his habit was, his nerves on edge, he drew back the curtains to peer out. What he saw there in the moonlight, very lovely and unearthly upon the snow, made him draw back in terror. There was no sleep for him that night ; he fancied he had seen the stone — which, as you know, was a couple of fields away — as large as life, as if it were on watch outside his window.

" Of course, it was just the disordered fancy of a child. He said not a word of what he suffered, but wrote down what he at any rate was convinced of in the journal he kept. But he never slept in that room again. It was shut up. He moved upstairs to a little attic room under the roof, with a dormer window that looked to the west.

"Nothing happened any more for a few days. He fancied he was safe. He took his mind off his obsession and turned to his music. He began to forget the scare he had had. It is dangerous to forget.

"One night he went to have a bath before going up to bed. The bath-room was at the back of the house and looked to the north. There was just enough light for him to see, and he was lying full length humming some theme that had occurred to him that evening, trying it out various ways in his head, when he looked up casually to see a long gaunt finger of shadow resting upon the window from outside. He turned cold with horror. Grabbing his dressing-gown he fled upstairs to the safety of his room.

"But now he knew that he was no longer safe wherever he was. The bath-room looked to the north; the long-stone stood in the fields to the east of the house. He could no longer console himself with the thought that it was an hallucination. He longed to leave the house; he hated the thought of the shadow that lay upon it and about it, that laid siege to it on every side. But he was afraid — afraid to confess that he was afraid, and so held on.

"The very next day he ran into Mrs. Chynoweth out walking again.

"'You don't seem to look very well,' she said in her breezy, familiar way. She was dressed as usual in dark heavy tweed with a man's soft felt hat worn slightly on one side. She carried a walking-stick with which she executed little cuts in the air; she was jauntier than ever. 'Cornwall not agreeing with you, perhaps? I shouldn't wonder, not in that house of yours with the name it's got with people here.'

"'What name?' said Christopher, surprised into indiscretion. So far as he was aware it was simply known as 'The Bungalow'.

"'Oh, people here call it "Longstone House".

24

Didn't you know what happened there a year or two ago with the last tenants who had the house ? They didn't tell you when you took it ? No, of course not. People are so secretive about things ; I can never understand why. Now I'm different ; I'm open ; I believe in being candid.'

" She certainly did. She didn't need Christopher's apprehensive invitation to tell him what had happened before plunging into her story.

" ' Well, it was very nasty for the time,' she said, ' and that was why the house stood empty until you came. There was a very nice couple that built the house just after the war. They came down here from London with their little girl. She was about ten or eleven — yes, eleven, the same age as my little girl. One evening just as it was getting dark she went down the drive to the gate — you know, where the path leads out into the road that comes from the longstone. She was found there a little later. They missed her from the house, and when they went down the drive there she was lying just outside her own gate. It was supposed that she had been knocked down by a passing lorry. But nobody had seen one. Nobody here believed that it was a lorry that was responsible. When they picked the poor little thing up, her right shoulder was shattered and there was a fracture of the right temple: just as if she had been lurched into by something very heavy. And believe me, it wasn't a car that did it.

" ' Now I don't know if you are interested in spiritualism, Mr. Wilford——'

" Christopher did not need her assurance, and the thought of her philosophising on the subject after what he had been through himself was more than he could bear. He took to his heels and unashamedly fled back to the house.

" That night alone he sat up late to listen in to a

concert he particularly wanted to hear, for it included the Fourth Symphony of Sibelius, the most monolithic of them all. He shut himself in the dining-room of the house, a room with heavy brocade curtains across the big window that looked due south. He had his journal out before him, into which he poured his soul : all his fears, agonies, all the things he felt he could share with no one : all written in pell-mell as if he had no time to spare — nor had he, poor lad ! — mixed up with musical themes jotted down, which he was trying out for some work that he wanted to compose — there was the title: 'Campo dei Morti'.

"As he listened, everything seemed to become un-naturally clear to him ; there was the inevitability of fate in the great marching strides of the basses in the first movement, very low, menacing steps coming nearer and nearer, which nothing could stop. In all this stony waste of sound, no tenderness, no sweetness, until at the moment of sacrifice the flutes sounded clear like human voices, wringing a certain sweetness out of the very stone, the heart of stone. Then there came the shrill insistent lament of violins, that pathetic motif of protest against the menacing rhythm of those monolithic steps. As he listened and wrote, his nerves on edge, a sixth sense rather than any reason told him that the moment had come, that the long striding steps of the basses in the music led in the world of space out through the window, that beyond the curtains there was that waiting for him to which all his brief life had been a pilgrimage. In short, if he tore open the curtains there would be the stone waiting for him.

"He could bear the suspense no longer, but flung back the curtains, threw open the window — at least that's the way it seems he must have gone — rushed down the drive to the gate, the way the little girl had gone before him, and along the path to where the stone awaited him. It would seem that that stone had a hunger for what was young and innocent.

" It was not until the early hours of the morning that they found him, lying like a sacrificial offering at the foot of the socket he had ventured to uncover. His right shoulder was crushed and the whole right side of his face was bruised and grazed as in some embrace that had been too strong for him. They found him in the grey light of a morning moon : an old moon, a rind of a moon upon its back in the west, which turned the whole landscape into death's kingdom and lit his face with a strange glimmer there where it lay at the stone's foot."

The Dean's story had come to an end. His eyes shone with an unusual intensity, as if he were more concerned by it than he cared to admit. Just before the end the electric light had come on again, with something of a shock ; so that the end of the story had been told in the hard glitter of unaccustomed light in their eyes, while the candles wavered their rather ghostly light on the mantel-piece. Nobody said anything for a moment. Then the young English don recited half aloud, half to himself :

> This ae nighte, this ae nighte,
> —Every nighte and alle,
> Fire and fleet and candle-lighte,
> And Christe receive thy saule.

Shortly afterwards, with a few brief words and Christmas greetings, they dispersed severally to their beds.

ALL SOULS' NIGHT

THEY were sitting — the Dean and two of his colleagues — in the quiet of a summer evening upon the terrace of that college, that quadrangle which gives you a panorama of the spire of St. Mary's, with its gathered pinnacles clustered at the base, the light and classical elegance of Aldrich's spire of All Saints in the background, the bulky Roman magnificence of the Radcliffe Camera in the foreground, and away to the innumerable crockets and finials of the Bodleian Library. It was that hour of summer evening when the late light lit up the clock upon the northern face of St. Mary's tower : a rare and disturbing thing to the hearts of those few whose attention was caught by it. Somehow it brought home to them, in an inexpressible way, the feeling of the transcendence of things, the mutability of the temporal order, the immutability of the eternal.

Nine was striking upon all the brazen tongues of the clocks of Oxford. There was the old-lady-stepping-upstairs chime of New College that began the clamour, followed by the lugubrious descent and ascent of St. Mary's, like going down into the tomb. Last of all, the deliberate, suspensive, velvety boom of Tom from Christ Church.

> Midnight has come, and the great Christ Church bell
> And many a lesser bell sound through the room ;
> And it is All Souls' Night . . .

the words ran through the dreamy mind of the young English don, while his attention wandered from the desultory conversation the Dean was having with his senior colleague, the Classic.

The Fellows had had their coffee in the open air, so

warm was the evening. And now, replete, at leisure, these three were enjoying the evening air, the Classic his pipe, the Dean his cigar. When the youngest of them next attended, his colleague was asking the Dean :

" By the way, what was it that overtook young Colenso ? I remember he was a lad of considerable promise as an undergraduate — great things were expected of him when he was elected to his Fellowship. I never really rightly understood what came of him. I dare say you know, my dear Dean : wasn't he one of your West-Country clientèle ? "

This was the regular phrase with which they teased the Dean about the interest he took, the almost fatherly interest, in the long file of young men coming up to the University from the West Country, from scholarship candidates to D.Phil. researchers. Anybody of West-Country connections had a claim upon his attention, if not upon his affections.

" Well, in a manner of speaking, he was," said the Dean. Then, after a pause, unhurriedly savouring his cigar, turning it round on his lips :

" There was no mystery about it, you know. It is quite clear what happened." He laid emphasis upon " what happened ", as if there were some mystery *before* what had happened.

" Poor fellow, he's still alive, though in a bad way, I gather."

(A ghost may come ;

— mused the abstracted, ruminating mind of the young English don —

For it is a ghost's right,
His element is so fine
Being sharpened by his death,
To drink from the wine-breath
While our gross palates drink from the whole wine.

But it wasn't the poor fellow of the Dean's acquaintance who was the ghost, he reflected. Perhaps he had seen a ghost ? He sat up and began to attend in earnest.)

" No, there was no mystery attached to it," the Dean was saying. " But it was certainly a very curious story.

" You see, I knew the lad — or rather the part of Cornwall he comes from — well. His was a sweet nature, a charming disposition ; and very level - headed and sensible, too. He was the last person you would have expected to——" He paused to inspect the end of his cigar, to see if it were properly alight.

" Expected to what ? " said the eager young Fellow, a little tense.

The Dean took no notice, went on his unhurried way. " He had got here on his own steam, won a lot of scholarships. He was quite capable of looking after himself. He hadn't much of a family in the background. I believe there was a father, who had gone off to America, or something of the sort, leaving the mother to fend for herself. The lad was brought up largely by his sister, who was much older than he was, ten or fifteen years. She was more of a mother to him.

" Up here young Colenso (Tristram was his name : rather curious, too — I believe it ran in the family), well, he did very well, got his first and was elected to a Research Fellowship almost at once. Perhaps it was rather a rush, a bit too much for him ; it may have overtaxed his strength. Better that these things should come slowly — let them ripen in due season," said the Dean, who had had several set-backs in his early academic career and thought it a good principle for everybody else that things should not come to them too easily.

" But he had to get something, poor lad," he added kindly. " And he had a very good subject for research right on his own doorstep, so to speak. You know the old Cornish family, the Lantyans, of Carn Tyan, who were

the greatest landowners in Cornwall in the Middle Ages
— though they have lost a good deal of their property
there since. They were absentees from the county for a
long time, from the sixteenth century to the eighteenth.
They were Catholics, and during the years of Elizabeth's
war with Spain they were not allowed to live in so dangerous an area, so remote from the centre, so near the sea,
and with the sympathies of their peasantry all Catholic
like their own. It was for them a prohibited area — as
for strangers today. How little things change in human
affairs ! " (The Dean enjoyed a good ripe platitude as it
might be a peach or a nectarine.) " Well, the Lantyans
have gone on being Catholic in an unbroken tradition —
and very proud they are of the fact. They say that in
their chapel at Carn Tyan there is a lamp that has
never been allowed to go out since the Reformation.

" The old Lady Lantyan bore an extraordinary character
in those parts. Jane Lucinda : she was the last representative of the Blanchminsters who owned a great deal
of land in North Cornwall in the Middle Ages, and
also one half, the secular half, of the Scilly Islands. The
old lady was a regular termagant, a well-known character
all over the West Country. For one thing she had
a terrific temper ; was immensely family - proud and
haughty ; a dominating old woman who lived to be
ninety and led her household and servants and everybody near her the devil of a life. Particularly, for some
odd reason, her chaplains. She seemed to hate them ;
she certainly persecuted them. Yet it never occurred
to her to dispense with them : there always had been a
priest in the household, and she simply couldn't conceive of a house without one — for her. It may be that
she wanted somebody or something to torment. She
had no children. Her husband had died years before,
leaving her in control of the money. So she remained on
in possession, keeping her heir, an elderly cousin of her

husband's, at arm's length. He couldn't have afforded to dispossess her anyway ; he was entirely dependent on her for what would, or might, come to him after her death.

" So she lived on at Carn Tyan, tormenting priests her chief pleasure in life, you might say. One after the other they left her, driven to distraction. One poor man, the last of them, a French priest, a cultivated, quiet, melancholy sort of man, who already seemed to have enough on his mind — as if there was a something in the background — was driven over the edge. He became stark raving mad. To begin with, she starved them. It wasn't that she was mean. It was just that she had very odd views about diet. She lived on next to nothing herself, with the aid — it is true — of the very best old cognac, such as she had a good store of in her cellars. You never come across brandy like that nowadays." The Dean gave a heartfelt sigh.

" The old lady was immensely aristocratic ; she couldn't believe but what suited her very well must be good for everybody else. She fed her priests mostly on rice and currants, relieved with brandy at every meal to wash it down. She insisted that to keep your health you had to drink brandy five times a day. Such of them as survived the endless rice and currant puddings became hopeless topers on the brandy. The combination was too much for her last priest. But then he had something else on his mind.

" Not that that much worried the old tartar, Jane Lucinda. Protest after protest at her treatment of her priests had been made by her bishop, the Bishop of Lysistrata. Without the slightest effect. At last a writ of excommunication was made out to be served upon her. Did that defeat her ? Not a bit of it. On the threshold of ninety, she called for her carriage and at once drove off to a Carmelite convent the other side of the county, to enter upon a long retreat, leaving instructions that on no

account should any correspondence be forwarded. So
that the writ never reached her. When the bishop at
length learned where she was, she left for the house of
a relation in Worcestershire. By the time it reached
Worcestershire she was in London. For the bishop it was
a regular wild-goose chase, making him look ridiculous
in the eyes of the whole Catholic community who knew
perfectly well what was going on. I believe the old
termagant thoroughly enjoyed the last months of her life.
Having outwitted her ecclesiastical superiors, she took to
her bed at her town house in London and died still
officially at peace with the Church, and fortified with all
the accustomed rites.

"At last her cousin, the thirteenth baronet — an
elderly man of sixty — entered into possession of the
almost derelict estate, a great house in which nothing had
been changed since the eighteen-sixties. He was the last
of the family. Like many another bachelor who had
himself done nothing to keep going the succession, he was
interested in his family history. And on coming into
possession, he found a muniment room stuffed full of old
deeds and documents, letter-books and papers, and wanted
some help in going through them. This is where young
Tristram Colenso came in. Sir Richard had heard of
his expertise in deciphering medieval handwritings, and
the idea was that he should write a family history of the
Lantyans and Blanchminsters. After all, the least the
baronet could do for posterity, since he hadn't produced
any issue of his own to continue it — so far as we are
aware ; at any rate not any legitimate issue," the Dean
added cautiously.

"So young Colenso was invited down for a week-end
to take a preliminary look through the papers in the
muniment room. It was his first experience of stopping
in a great country house — and alas, poor lad, I suppose
it will be his last. He was very excited and impressed.

All very natural. He had heard of Carn Tyan all his life, but had never so much as set eyes on it.

"The house is in a very remote and un-get-at-able part of Cornwall — the Tamar Valley. Also one of the most lovely, with a singular fascination of its own. You know, my dear Done, how people up here are liable to say, 'Of course the coast of Cornwall is very beautiful, but the county has no interior.' What nonsense it is!" The Dean, a very patriotic Cornishman, grew quite angry. "Just the impression of ignorant tourists rushing through the county along the main motor-road to New-quay or St. Ives or the Lizard. As a matter of fact, all the river valleys are extremely beautiful country : Hel-ford, the country of the Fal, the Fowey, the Camel, and not least, the Tamar. In spite of Plymouth being at its gate, the Tamar country is the most unspoiled, as it is the least accessible."

Having made his point, the Dean sent the junior Fellow into the smoking-room to get him a whisky-and-soda, and on his return resumed the story. Meanwhile they watched the last rosy flush of light catching the topmost cupola of the Radcliffe Camera. The Dean's colleague, the Classic, thought of the lovely orange-and-rose flush in the sky of Rome as you look from the Pincio Gardens to the dome of St. Peter's in the west across the darkening spaces of the city. Yes, he thought, the Camera is the most Roman thing in Oxford — and as good as anything in Rome. Fortified by his whisky-and-soda, the Dean resumed.

"When Colenso arrived at the station at Launceston after an all-day journey, there was a car to meet him. They drove for miles through the failing light — it was the very beginning of November — until he recognised the long serrated crest of the woods, the nearest he had ever been to the house, upon the next ridge. It was not without a thrill that he passed through the gates, the pillars sur-

mounted by lions upholding shields, the arms of the
Lantyans, and into the grand gloom of the park. He
just caught sight of the splendid fans of the cedars upon
the lawn when they drove up to the front door.

" His first impression was of the magnificence of the
great double staircase which swept down its marble arms
into the hall. He was shown up to his room by a maid
carrying a little hand lamp through the vast and shadowy
gloom. At the head of the staircase there were at least
eight great mahogany doors in a semicircle. They went
through one on the right and along an unfinished corri-
dor, through several large rooms, of which one was a
book-room, and down a little curved passage to his own
door. It opened into a huge state-bedroom, with great
state-bed under a canopy at the farther end. His heart
sank a little at the spectacle : it was altogether too grand
for him, he thought. He felt that it was a mistake, his
coming.

" Opening a note the maid had given him, he found
that it was from Sir Richard, regretting that he couldn't
be there to receive him. He had had to go urgently into
Plymouth that afternoon and hoped to be back in time
for dinner at eight. Tristram had plenty of time to look
round and dress at leisure. He was evidently expected to
occupy this room : there was a wood fire lit for him in
the Adam fireplace. It burnt up cheerfully. But the
room was far too large to be cheerful in itself. Fancy
sleeping in a bedroom that had a couple of columns at
each end, thought Tristram ; in a state-bed large enough
for four. How does one sleep in it ? he wondered ; does
one sleep on the outer edge, or leap boldly into the
middle ?

" He looked round by the light of the lamp and the
candles lighted on the dressing-table. No electricity
anywhere. The room gave an impression of the gloomy
splendour of a former age, rather than of opulence in this.

There were eighteenth-century portraits on the wall, and beautiful things about : silver candlesticks on dressing-table and writing-table, and a smaller one for the hand with snuffers beside the bed. All very well, he thought, but no electric light to turn on, if you should want it in the night.

" With time on his hands he settled down to write the journal-letter that he wrote to his sister when anything special happened to him, such as going away on a visit. Then it was time for him to change. He put on his newly starched shirt and trousers and silk socks, arranged his studs and cuff-links, when he discovered that he had forgotten to bring a dress tie. The kind of accident that happens to us all, when we are young," said the Dean sympathetically, with a memory of some similar mis-adventure to himself before he had lost his youthful diffidence. " And what upsets us far worse than many things in themselves more important.

" Tristram was struck with horror. He had specially packed everything himself that morning so that nothing of the kind should happen. Young and inexperienced, he regarded this in the light of a major disaster. It took him a long time to summon up courage to ring the bell. It took an even longer time for the maid to answer his summons from somewhere in the depths of this vast, silent house. She came back with an old-fashioned tie of Sir Richard's, with his compliments.

" As the hour of eight approached he took his lamp and made his way back, not without some doubt and a few wrong turnings, to the head of the magnificent stair-case, and downstairs. Going under the arch into the small dining-room he saw a figure in a corner strenuously engaged in drawing a cork. He took him to be the butler. It was in fact Sir Richard, acting as butler himself.

" They shook hands and went into the dining-room together. Tristram was rather set at ease by the unexpected manner of their meeting, was made to feel completely at home by the way Sir Richard chaffed him about the tie — he said it was what he always did himself when *he* was young ; the young man ended by being quite conquered by his host's old-fashioned charm of manner. The baronet was very tall and good-looking, with crisp grey hair ; in spite of a gouty leg, he would himself get up to fetch Tristram a cigarette or ash-tray, or open the door. Sir Richard certainly knew how to render himself agreeable to the young scholar. During dinner there was a good deal of amusement at the expense of the departed dowager and her ways — fantastic stories of which Sir Richard had a whole repertoire. (She had her revenge, in her own way," commented the Dean.) " Tristram concluded that if the redoubtable Jane Lucinda were after an Elizabethan pattern, haughty and overbearing, like the famous Bess of Hardwick or Lettice Knollys, her successor the baronet was the perfection of eighteenth-century courtesy, easy and affable.

" The meal was very simple ; there was only one maid to wait at table. The baronet did his own butling. Though the silver was beautiful, Tristram couldn't but observe that the carpet was threadbare. Dinner ended with a couple of glasses of port from the bottle that Sir Richard had been caught in the act of decanting. He took it as a joke and made fun of his impoverished estate. None the less it was evident what a pride he had in his ancestry and everything that concerned his family's history. Tristram could hardly keep up with his refer-ences to the seventh or tenth Sir Richard or the heiresses who had brought in this or that estate in the distant past, or his way of thinking of English history as episodes in the more continuous and certain story of his family.

After dinner, taking their light with them, they went out and down through a stone passage to the muniment room. It was a young researcher's paradise. So many cupboards and presses and chests of drawers, boxes and trunks and iron deed-boxes, crammed full of old documents — most of them medieval, it seemed. There were rent-rolls and accounts, copies of inquisitions, terriers and fines, duplicates of wills, letters and letter-books — all in the most agreeable confusion. Many a day's pleasant work for a couple of enthusiastic antiquarians. But the box which most tickled Tristram's intuitive sense as a researcher — his nose for documents : a sort of sixth sense — was locked and the key lost. Nothing would induce it to open. They tried all the keys, but none would fit the lock. It was most provoking, for from the lettering outside Tristram could see that it contained documents relating to the most interesting of Cornish monastic houses. He tried various little keys of his own upon the lock, but only succeeded in breaking them and leaving their heads in the wards.

" It was after eleven when they gave up, and Sir Richard accompanied his guest up the grand staircase to his room. The fire was burning brightly, throwing elongated shadows across the high ceiling. Tristram got into bed, keeping to the edge of it ; there was an interminable space unoccupied the other side of him, he thought. He was surprised at the bed's comfort. He put out his light and tried to settle himself to sleep. But there was still the firelight and those long wavering shadows like fingers pointing across the room at him. Whether it was the port, or the excitement of the muniment room, his head was in a whirl. He was just falling asleep, when the thought of Lady Lantyan's French priest came into his mind. He had gone mad in this house, perhaps in this very room.

" After that, there was no sleep for Tristram. He lay there for a bit, his heart beating audibly beneath the bedclothes of the great bed, listening, straining his ears to catch every sound in the vast silence, an owl hooting outside in the park, the swish-swish — what was it ? — of the twigs of a tree against the window-pane. Unable to bear it any longer, unable to sleep, he lit his candle, got out, put on his dressing-gown, and went to the writing-table to take refuge in the comfort of writing to his sister.

" It was the worst thing he could have done, probably ; writing only heated his imagination the more, stimulated his nervous sensibility, made him doubly aware of every sound and movement.

" I don't quite know what happened next ; one can only piece it together from his account of that night afterwards. He was never very sure of the order in which things happened, even at his best. And, of course — at the worst——" The Dean paused, finished his whisky-and-soda, and went on :

" It seems that he was looking for something to read, something to take back to bed with him. I don't know whether there were any books in the room ; he may have gone out through the little passage into the book-room to find something. Or he may have found it in the drawer of that writing-table. Wherever it was, with the unfailing flair of the born researcher — which he undoubtedly had, poor fellow — he put his hand on a little manuscript book that had belonged to the French priest."

The Dean stopped and lit a cigarette to keep off the gnats which were beginning to pester him, like a cloud of disagreeable memories that one wants to exorcise.

" That little manuscript book, a sort of diary, gave the clue to the secret of the French priest. He had an irre-mediable sin upon his conscience, which tormented him and turned his life into agony. Apparently he had been in his early years left with the charge of a small child, a boy, whose parents were his near relations. He regarded this charge with distaste, as a burden upon his career (he was poor and ambitious). In his early years he did the minimum he could for this child, had him placed in an

39

orphanage and barely kept touch with his responsibility. Some dozen or fifteen years later he received a message to come to the bedside of his young relation. The lad was now in a seminary.

" The priest found that his uninteresting charge had grown into a youth, intelligent and of great charm — but, alas, far gone in consumption. Touched to the heart at last, but too late, he remained there with him all through that summer and autumn. Until, in fact, the end. The boy died on All Souls' Day, the second of November.

" Every day for the rest of his life when All Souls' Day came round the priest said a requiem for him. When he came to Carn Tyan, as All Souls'-tide approached, he became more and more plunged into profound gloom. An inconsolable misery seemed to possess him, turning him inwards upon himself. During that period he was in the habit of inflicting on himself austerities, which left him in a mingled state of physical exhaustion and mental excitement. It was really the first symptom of his madness. He thought himself responsible for the death of his young charge. This was his retribution.

" As Tristram picked up the threads of this story of suffering and penance, this confession of guilt from a dead man, something of the priest's state of morbid excitement communicated itself to him. He was already in a very susceptible condition : the strangeness of the house, the excitement of the muniments, the listening silences of the great room in which sleep was now impossible.

" The fire had burned down to a last occasional flicker, making more absolute the shadows in all the room, save for the patch of light by the bedside.

" What was that that stirred at the farther end of the room ? Tristram listened with every nerve in his body on edge. In the confusion of his senses he could not tell whether it was something that registered itself to the sense of sight or hearing. He sat up, listening, peering between the great bed-posts into the darkness. The sound came more distinctly from that direction : it was something like a low moan. He listened : the strange hoarse sibilance became clearer : it was a pattern, a mutter of words. But the words did not seem to make sense.

" At last Tristram caught quite distinctly the words, ' mea culpa, mea culpa, mea maxima culpa ', uttered with an inexpressible anguish such as he thought no human voice could attain. Tristram wasn't a Catholic ; he had been brought up an Anglican, a rather High Church Anglican. He recognised the Confession of the priest at the beginning of the Canon of the Mass. The Latin words were spoken with an unmistakable French accent.

" With all his senses alive, his nerves on edge, he watched intently : it was as if he saw everything in the room at once, out of the corners of his eyes. Sitting up in bed looking straight before him to the other end of the room, upon which his fears were concentrated, he suddenly saw the great door behind him at *this* end of the room open softly, slowly on its hinges, as if for someone to pass through. He was transfixed there, waiting. Nobody. Nobody passed through. The great door closed as noiselessly, as slowly as it had opened.

" But was there nobody that had passed through ? A sense of unutterable grief, of inconsolable suffering, had invaded the room. It was unnerving. Tristram could stand it no longer.

" Hardly knowing what he was doing, he got out of bed and out of the room at the other end to find himself in darkness outside. His brain was working with the unnatural clarity that goes with such an experience ; all his apprehensive senses were aroused by what was about him. He realised, quite rationally, with the disjunctive logic of a dream, that the reason for the curve in the passage leading to the great room was that it was here the end of the chapel abutted on to the house ; and he found himself looking down from the family pew high up in the gallery at the west end of the building upon the scene that enacted itself below.

" He had no doubt about what was going on down there. There were the shadowy figures, vested, before the altar; upon the altar itself the two candles of the rubric. Fascinated, unable to move from the spot, he heard the immemorial Roman mutter, the introit of the Mass for the Dead :

> Requiem aeternam dona eis, Domine, et lux perpetua
> luceat eis.

It seemed to him that he heard the strange toneless voices articulating the *Dies Irae* from the beginning :

> Dies irae, dies illa
> Solvet saeclum in favilla,
> Teste David cum Sibylla

to the very end :

> Judicandus homo reus :
> Huic ego parce, Deus.
> Pie Jesu, Domine,
> Dona eis requiem.

His eyes were so fixed upon the figures round the altar, that it was only when the whimper of the *Dies Irae* was over that he noticed in the gloom before the sanctuary that there was a catafalque, with one taper, no more than a rushlight, burning at the head. It was a small coffin, very slender and shapely. Then he knew whose requiem it was that was proceeding down below.

" With that thought there came over him a sense of inextinguishable grief such as had passed through the great room. Only now it seemed to invade him by every crevice open to its penetration, eyes, ears, mouth, throat. Overwhelmed with a grief that was not his, he stumbled back into the room, lit the candles one by one, every one of them, upon writing-table, dressing-table, at the bed-side. If there had been a hundred candles, still he would have lit them all to lighten the oppression weighing upon his spirits.

" He sat down before the dressing-table, face plunged in hands. It was when he removed his hands for a moment that he noticed something strange about his appearance. There were creases, there were lines upon his face, at the corners of mouth and nostrils, around the eyes. It seemed to him that the more he looked, the more lined his face became. It was like the face of someone else. But above all it was the eyes that arrested his attention. His eyes were dark ; but the eyes that fixed him in the mirror were grey and steely, with that strange fanatic quality you sometimes see in Frenchmen's eyes. As he watched, the whole face began to twitch : it was the face of a madman.

" In the morning when it was daylight, they found him still seated there before the mirror, gibbering."

THE BENEFICENT SHOES

EVERYBODY said they were a very nice young couple. And so they were. They were, as everyone remarked, ideally suited to each other. They were both school teachers. They had met at Plymouth, where he had been a master in a big boys' secondary school, while she was a mistress in the girls'. So they had that community of interest which everyone assures us is the foundation of a successful marriage.

Not less important, they were in other respects mutually complementary. She was the active, practical spirit who managed the house and, in effect, their joint career. But she had decided to subordinate her own career to his : when he obtained the headship of a small secondary school in mid-Cornwall, she married him.

He was the more interesting character, though a less good teacher. Where she was direct and forcible, with a clear head and way of explaining things, he was diffident and oblique in his approach — an unsympathetic observer would say at first, a little confused. Which was not quite true : it was just that he was aware, perhaps, of more things at once than either Jane or the unsympathetic observer. He had a natural distinction of mind, which somehow his curious fits of absent-mindedness did not impair, but rather enhanced. And there went along with this an unmistakable goodness of nature, a sympathy of temper which could be felt rather than expressed.

Not that Jane had not a real goodness of heart too, but hers was a thoroughly practical nature. She was English. He was Cornish — or rather half-Cornish, which added to the indecisions, the impreciseness of his mind, and perhaps accounted for those quivering antennae of sensibility which were not easily observable to some people.

He came of farmer stock and had a good Cornish name : Dennis Tristain. (One wishes Cornish people would draw more upon the lovely names they have coming down from their remote past : Mark, Gawain, and Tristram ; Perran, Petrock, and Geraint.)

They had already settled into a house which suited them very well. It was not an old house — one of those dank, grey Cornish houses which are inevitably associated with the idea of ghosts. Jane would not have held with such ideas anyway. She would have regarded them as illusions, for which her practical mind had no use. Dennis — though he, too, if asked direct, would probably have agreed that they were illusions — instinctively knew the hidden truth, and with a native Cornish caution would have given the universe the benefit of the doubt.

Anyhow, their house, so far from being large and gloomy and at the end of a long, dark drive of rhododendrons and ilexes, was small and gay and at the end of a short straight drive in from the main road. It was built, like a good many modern houses in Cornwall, after a manner brought back from overseas, from South Africa or Michigan or Montana, with which Cornish folk have had so many mining connections in the past : that is to say, it was practically a bungalow, with verandahs all round. Very agreeable, since it had a good view of the sea, with the lizard-like neck of the headland, as of some great primitive animal, closing their seaward view.

All that they knew of the history of the house was that it had been built by a mining captain, who had returned having " made his fortune ", but with the hand of the miners' phthisis heavy upon him. The captain was a laconic bachelor of whom people knew little ; he had been looked after by an elderly " person ", a little lame, who kept herself very much to herself and was his housekeeper. He died, and she died shortly after.

The house was so up-to-date that it had not even a

horseshoe over the door — as every Cornish house should
have — to bring its inmates good luck, as we say nowadays, or, as the older folk know, to keep witches out.
Dennis a little regretted this, as he had a feeling for the
ancient ways of his people ; but he knew that any attempt
to rectify the omission would be regarded with little
patience by Jane. So the house went unprotected.

Jane liked it there : it was a pleasurable experience to
direct her undoubted talent for running things (and
people) into a new channel. Dennis afforded her plenty
of scope. He was the untidiest person in the world : a
charming disorder naturally arose all round him. Books
piled themselves up on the floor wherever he was ; papers,
newspapers, journals, reports accumulated on his writing-
desk and so snowed him under that there was no writing
at it ; the particular paper he was in need of at the
moment had a way of hiding itself in the mass, into which
Dennis would plunge hopelessly, helplessly, a puzzled look
in those sloe-black eyes with the curious almond shape.
Jane was very fond of him, especially at such moments :
she took him in hand. She had a favourite epitaph for
him, with which she used to tease him ; there would be
found inscribed upon his tombstone, she said, the words
" He never shut a drawer ".

In some months of married life Dennis was making
good progress in the art of shutting drawers and replacing
books on shelves, when his incurable forgetfulness seemed
to break out in another direction. He could never be
sure where he had put his shoes : they always seemed to
be turning up somewhere other than where he thought he
had left them.

" Where have you put my shoes, darling ? " he would
say sweetly, wandering rather disconsolately round the
house after Jane.

" I haven't seen them," she would say. And then
add : " Anyone would think that they had walked off

of themselves — the way you mislay them about the place."

Dennis did indeed think there was something odd about the way they turned up in the most unexpected corners, where he felt he had never left them. But he owned many pairs of shoes, large and comfortable, mostly rather old and well-worn, inclined to be a bit " trolled-over ", as we say ; and he could never be *quite* sure : he knew his own absent-minded ways too well. So he said nothing to Jane, who would have laughed at him for his pains.

When the confusion became too insistent to avoid notice, she introduced a rule. Dennis was to keep his shoes in order in the back kitchen — that is to say, those pairs which he wasn't using at the moment.

One day, not long after this measure of reform, Dennis came home from school, changed into his slippers in the kitchen, leaving his out-door shoes there, went down to their bedroom for a book, read for a little, wandered into his study and out again into the sitting-room, where a cheerful fire was burning and Jane had the tea ready — to find that his shoes were waiting for him beside his drawn-up chair in front of the fire.

" Thank you, darling," he said. " I didn't know that they were wet."

" What is ? " said Jane, her mind concentrated on pouring out tea with one hand and fetching out a plate of hot scones with the other.

" My shoes," said he contentedly, helping himself to a scone.

" But, my dear, I haven't touched them," said Jane, paying attention once more.

" You must have done," said Dennis, opening incredulous eyes.

Jane caught the look in his eyes, and answered shortly, " What nonsense ! You know perfectly well you must have put them there yourself to dry."

" I did not," he began ; " I could swear that I took them off in the kitchen and left them there." Having said as much for himself, he then began to wonder. Had he after all taken them off in the kitchen ? The strange chord deep down in his consciousness — something lost in his early experience — which was aroused whenever he contemplated his own forgetfulness, vibrated with uncertainty. He was no longer sure. Perhaps he had taken his shoes off in the bedroom and brought them up with him ? But he distinctly remembered sitting down on a chair in the kitchen and taking them off there. On the other hand, that might have been yesterday. What was he doing yesterday ? His mind, wandering down those familiar corridors of the research into memory, lost control of the situation.

Jane, with her woman's instinct, realised that and resumed it into her own hands. She said affectionately, " Really, darling, anybody would think it was someone else walking round the house in your shoes."

He was defeated. She made the defeat palatable by handing him the plate in her most seductive manner : " Denny, dear, have another scone. They're a great success today. I'm really rather proud of them."

He looked down at the shoes. They looked up at him in a faithful, mute, protesting way, as if to say they were at his service, however much they might be disregarded, discountenanced, in other quarters.

He understood the look. It was lost on her. At the same moment he had that curious experience which we all know well : of having been through it all before on some previous occasion. He felt, as he sat there, that he had been sitting there before just like that, wrangling with Jane about those shoes ; there was the plate of scones, there were the shoes looking up at him, the same thought passing through his head, and he had heard her — oh so clearly, so insistently, before — saying just those words :

" *Anybody would think it was someone else walking round the house in your shoes.*"

Though his was a poetical mind, it was also not without logic ; and he found himself thinking : " But the shoes were not wet at all, so I couldn't have put them there to dry."

He was now quite certain in himself. But he said nothing to Jane : there were things that that admirable clear mind could not conceive. It was the first time that he perceived at all clearly its limitations. He had been content to repose entirely upon her practical capacity, her better judgment. He was now not so sure. This was the first time they had had anything approaching a tiff. She had won, as was to be expected ; but all the same, she was not right. It was a very small matter ; but it is precisely upon such small matters that a widening rift in sympathies is revealed. The matter dropped between them.

Some months later Dennis' sister was married from the house. (She was his only sister, and their parents were no longer alive.)

Jane was absolutely at her best in these proceedings, took charge of her sister-in-law, made most of the arrangements about her trousseau, and, with the aid of her faithful attendant Mrs. Honey — whose sole ambition in life was to have her good Cornish name, which we all know how to pronounce, pronounced Hony to rhyme with bony, stony, or phoney — cooked the wedding luncheon. Jane entered thoroughly into the spirit of a Cornish wedding, and was willing to aid Judy in her determination not to omit a single customary propriety. The bride, according to custom, must wear one piece of clothing which was old and another which was borrowed. Mrs. Honey produced an old garter and Jane lent Judy a petticoat for the occasion.

Dennis, for his part, was determined not to omit the proper rite of throwing an old shoe for luck after the departing couple.

They lingered long over their excellent luncheon ; and when the car finally drove off down the drive on the way to their honeymoon, the winter's day was drawing in. It was growing dark. Dennis followed the car down to the gates, and as it turned in the main road, took a good straight aim with his old shoe. The shoe hit the back wheel hard and rebounded like a boomerang. A hand-kerchief waved from the car, the white ribbons fluttered ; they were off and away.

What followed was quite incredible. It was incredible to Dennis, who could hardly believe his own eyes. He was acquainted with the theory of boomerangs ; he was interested in folklore. But neither of these interests had prepared him to see that shoe returning up the drive with him. It was between the two lights ; it was growing darker every second. But there was enough light for Dennis to see that the shoe was not travelling in a straight line like a boomerang, but that it was trudging faithfully, convincingly up the drive step by step, as if alternating with another step that could not be seen : the shuffling gait of a tired elderly person, which was yet indefatigable, undiscouraged. There was something touching about that solitary step. One would say it was the walk of a woman, a little lame.

Dennis was not exactly frightened, for there was no-thing malevolent about it : rather the contrary, it gave an impression of an unwearying, an unselfish devotion — something wholly beneficent. Yet he felt all his sensi-bilities become acute and tingling ; his nerves thrilled ; he felt that unmistakable sensation you have when your hair begins to rise and stand up on end. Never had he taken a walk that was so long as those few steps up the drive. Yet he could do nothing, did not wish to do anything. It was just as if he had been mesmerised.

When he got back to Jane and they went indoors together, she could see that something very odd had happened to him. And this time he told her, without any reserve.

She looked at him for a bit, and then burst into a peal of sound hearty laughing :

" Denny, darling," she said, " d'you know, you are quite, *quite* tight."

She thought him, helpless as he was, utterly charming. Nothing would persuade her to the contrary — she was that sort of woman ; nothing but ocular demonstration. And that was not very long in coming.

A fortnight after the wedding, on Twelfth Night, they were thinking of going down to the little church — the spire could be seen among the trees between the house and the sea — where a Nativity play was to be performed in place of the usual evensong. They were in a hurry to put the tea-things away, and had almost finished when they saw something very odd indeed. They quite distinctly saw a pair of Dennis' shoes walk slowly but doggedly across the room to the corner where they were washing up — pause, as if expecting some notice to be taken, and then return to where they had started from.

Their hearts stood still. They looked at each other ; it was as if the scales had fallen from Jane's eyes and she saw further into the depths of Dennis' personality than she had ever seen before. She felt, for the first time, uncertain of herself, horribly uncertain. She went very pale and thought for a moment she was going to faint. She was visibly shaken. Dennis put an arm round her and led her into the sitting-room where she lay down for a bit on the sofa.

" What does it mean ? " were her first words when she came round and recovered her self-control.

" I don't know," was all Dennis could say. And then

he remembered that he had recognised the same character, the same personality (so to say) in the steps : far from malevolent — kindly, wanting to be of service, as of some woman, ageing, but unwearied in doing good.

" I'm sure they mean nothing bad to us," he added. " Did you notice one thing about them, darling ? They were the steps of someone a little lame ? "

Jane had noticed : there was nothing that she had not observed now that at last she had seen for herself. She was more than willing now to credit what had happened to Dennis in the drive on the evening of the wedding, and the other oddities that had occurred in his behaviour.

But what did it mean ? That was the question that bothered them both. They did not go to church that evening ; they stayed at home discussing it. They wanted to get it clear.

It was a decidedly queer experience ; nothing that they had come across — or even read of — corresponded with it. They were a modern-minded young couple, intellectually open to conviction ; and they were quite *au fait* with ghost stories — liked them in a superior way, a sort of pleasant titillation of the imagination.

It had never occurred to either of them to credit that *these things might happen.* They were willing to go as far as to allow that there might be something in an atmosphere. Where people had been through an intense experience, had been very unhappy, for example, that might leave some impress of the experience in the atmosphere of a room, a house where it had taken place. What had not occurred to their minds was that the same might be true of a place or a house where someone had been very happy, to which someone was very attached. And that it might be something more than mere atmosphere.

Such was the upshot of their discussion. Not very satisfactory, and inconclusive, as all such discussions are.

A more practical upshot was that Jane was determined to leave the house.

Dennis was at bottom a little shocked that Jane, who had been so insentient, so unimaginative at first, should take it so badly when brought face to face with the facts. The facts were not at all frightening, he assured her. After all, it was certainly a benevolent ghost that haunted the house. It was the first time the word had been uttered between them. The assurance carried no weight with her. She was as obstinate now as she had been incredulous and positive at first. Was this a further widening in the rift of sympathy between them ?

Dennis gave way to her desire to leave the house. But before going, he determined to explore the facts as far as he could.

The facts were few. There was nothing very much to know. Merely that the previous occupant, a man dying slowly of the " miners' complaint ", had been looked after, people said, by a countrywoman who had come down there from the uplands — the great mass of moor and heath above the town. That she was a kindly person who, in spite of her lameness, dragged herself round to the last with cups of tea and hot-water bottles and medicine, fetching and carrying for the shy, reserved sort of man who treated her with respect and consideration. Never a complaint. She once told someone that the happiest years of her life were those she passed there. Hers had not been a happy life. She had been stricken with serious illness when young, which had left her lame. Her mother had made her give up the young man who wished to marry her — as a matter of duty. After her parents' death she had lived a lonely life on her small-holding up in the hills. It became too much for her to carry on by herself, and she came down to the town to seek employment. All that she wished was to help others, and that she did until she died.

These were the facts, few and simple and kindly. But what was the explanation?

In this realm where there are no explanations, one can only ask questions. If only the young couple were wise enough to let her ghost help them in her way? . . . Was that what she wished? Since they were not, must she still go dragging her steps around those passages, until someone comes who will understand and accept unquestioning and without apprehension the willing service of those faithful feet?

RESTINNES? RESTINNES?

IT happened to me the other day — what I had often
hoped for in vain before — to be lost within a few
miles of my home. The Cornish have an expression
for such an experience — and indeed the experience
itself was in the old days well known enough : it is to be
" pisky-laden ". But all the accounts that I have ever
heard of this curious happening agree that it takes place
at night, or at dusk-fall when the light is low. Somebody
returning from market in the town — it more often
happened, very curiously, in returning from somewhere
than in going — had to cross an open yet confined space
on their way, a patch of moor, more usually a field.
Somehow the person crossing would lose his sense of
direction ; the more sure he was that the way out was in
a certain place, the more that place would elude him.
It was as if he were being deliberately misled ; as if the
spirit of the place — and who can deny that certain
places have a spirit of their own ? —were leading him on,
mocking, in the end to make him a figure of fun. Round
and round he would go, getting more and more bothered,
all sense of direction now hopelessly lost, having double-
crossed his tracks a dozen times in the search for the way
out, not a little terrified in the dim light, the queer
alertness of the place, the whisperings of animate things,
the hour late : such an experience, he would say, certainly having come to him in some form — the storm-
lamp of a miner going on night-shift, or possibly (more
annoying), finding himself suddenly opposite the gate in
a most unexpected quarter — such it was to be " pisky-
laden ".

But there was no excuse for me, not being on my way
home from market, and in any case, a hopeless and con-

firmed teetotaller. Moreover, what happened to me was in the broad light of day, in the late afternoon, at my favourite tea-time hour. Perhaps there is something queer about that hour : I do not know : I sometimes think so.

However, I had set out from home skirting the side of the china-clay village, a heap of glistening sand, and crossing over the " Bottoms " — by which name we call the little valleys through which the china-clay streams run off their refuse sand to the sea — had passed through the evangelical village of Bethel, up the valley through Tregrehan Mills, and into that savage and desolate region which so expresses itself in its name, Garker. All this was known familiar country, walked over a hundred times, not more than a mile or two from home. But suddenly, hardly thinking where I was going, I was prompted to strike off up the hillside by a lane to the right, which I remembered having traversed only once before and then led to the curious half-ruined granite village of Trethurgy, on my way homeward. The lane was most promising : it ran steeply up the side of the hill with seductive little bends and curves, with glimpses across the intervening country to a blue arm of the sea, or back upon the valley with its grim harassed slopes, raked and washed for tin by countless generations of vanished miners. Here it looked down upon a little homestead in a clearing, its tiny shorn fields around the house, the poor shocks of wheat standing golden-brown in the late August sun. It was a lane to make one's heart rejoice, it was so very Cornish : here and there it ran deep between granite boulders ; the rough scrub country came right up to it on either side ; it was fringed by brambles, already glistening with black fruit. Another sharp bend, and it brought me straight into the farm-yard, or as we say in Cornwall the " town-plaace ", of a farm which I did not remember.

It was a substantial, Georgian-built farm-house of granite, a surprise in this poor rocky waste : a long fine front of five windows in the upper storey. It had stood there for centuries, for all around it were planted tall sheltering trees, mostly Cornish elms, some very old. Then I saw why : this was where the springs issued from the hill. There was abundance of water splashing into a row of great stone troughs below the house. This would be a settlement from early times : it must have a Celtic place-name of its own ; what would it be ? I wondered.

All was silent and sleepy about the house, save for the plashing of the water from the springs. I might have drawn some intimation from the mood the house was in. As I rounded it, I noticed that every window and every door in it, and they were many, was wide open, so many gaping mouths ; yet there was no sound inside the house and nobody looked from any of its windows. Was everybody in the house dead ? There were two tethered dogs in the yard by their kennels : they muttered a little at first, but made no more noise. By the barn-door was a litter of half-grown kittens, four black ones and three tabbies. I did not reflect till afterwards that that made seven.

I passed the house quickly, noting that I had never passed it before, and followed the lane out. The fields below fell very steeply into a valley : the corn had been carried in this one : there was the rick by the hedge, a large black cat lying in the straw at its foot. Above the lane, the fields sloped more gently up to the heights, in the direction I thought to come out. Soon, however, it came to an end in a gate and a field. Crossing this, keeping to the hedge (for I was now not sure of my way) I came to a patch of open downs, the tall bracken criss-crossed by the paths of beasts and men. There was a rickety gate to get over which threatened to break, in pieces beneath me : the end of the enclosed fields, I

E

considered, all now plain and open before me.

This was delicious. The place was open and fresh with the pure air from the higher downs. It was a meeting-place of gates, giving views backwards upon the valleys and the sea. Never was there such pure clear colour : after the late rain, the bay was of a deep blue, in swathes indigo ; the sky was washed, the great clouds towered broad-based upon the hills. My wits astray as I went, forgetting the present, I lost myself in the dream of history that this country upon the right has always meant for me since childhood. It was down the valley between those hills, along the course of the river Fowey, that King Charles came with his courtiers in pursuit of the Parliamentarian Army under Essex in 1644 : what a world was that ! An earlier, simpler, more gallant world : a world of romance to me, a child, with men on horseback foraging across this country ; a world when it was always early summer morning, the skies of a rare blue, camp-fires smoking on the edge of oak copses. Always in my childhood when I looked across to the Gribbin peninsula, I saw the figure of the King in black armour on his charger, occupying the whole horizon, that melancholy face with the long locks outlined against the sky. Other pictures too filled my mind, always of the Civil War : the dark pew in Boconnoc church where the King worshipped during that summer campaign ; the night when, frightened of conspiracy, he slept in his coach in the park surrounded by his guards ; the King's letter of thanks for the loyalty of Cornwall faithfully posted up in so many Cornish churches, the musty interiors, the moth-eaten curtains.

So ruminating, I found myself in quite different country : a patch of moor, which in Cornwall means, with more exact etymology, marshy ground, usually low-lying. For what other people would call moorland, the high stony wastes covered with gorse and bracken, we reserve the word " downs ".

The stretch of ground upon which I was now well embarked was even more fascinating than that I had left. This was sandy and dry, but with all sorts of runnels and channels that the rains had made coming down from the higher ground to these flats. To walk upon it was pure pleasure : it was so thickly covered with heath and ling and moor plants springy to the tread. The place had a character of its own, which came from its isolation, its separateness, for it was cut off practically all round by wilderness : that kind of no-man's-land of stunted trees, tall shrubs, and luxuriant vegetation which grows up wherever there is a catchment and water collects in the " bottoms " in the moorland districts of Cornwall.

But it was precisely this quality of separateness, and something more, which was not long in making its own queer impression on me, unconsciously. It was as if this place were something to itself, which I had broken into, not belonging to it ; as if it remained, therefore, with-drawn — one could feel an intake of the breath, on guard, watchful to make its own return. This curious impression quickened all the senses, to such an extent that the keenly-sensed pleasure of being there which first aroused me became with each minute a more fearful, a more pre-carious pleasure. The feeling was heightened by the fact that wherever I looked there seemed no way out ; which-ever track I took curiously melted into another, or ran round the enclosure without an issue, in any case ended in nothingness. Upon both sides was the barrier of the wilderness, in front reinforced by a stream which spread its marshy waters far beyond the high stone hedge, which as usual in Cornwall encircled the enclosure. The more anxious I became to break out of the place, to be back in time for tea — the hour was passing — the less chance of an opening in its defences appeared. One corner of the enclosed heath had a sinister appearance, it was so heavily overgrown with stunted oak and ash, a tangled under-

growth of brambles and gorse, that I failed to push my
way into it ; in any case, it was not in that direction that
I could get through to the friendly road.

What added paradox to the situation was that all the
time I knew the general geography of the country perfectly well. There were the familiar landmarks out in the
open country beyond : the granite tower of Luxulyan
church in the distance ; nearer by, on the high ground
in front, was the familiar shape of the sand-burrow of
Pentruff. That was all very well ; but how to get out?
I was not yet reduced to retracing my steps one by one
over the way I had come ; or in my agitation, it did not
occur to me.

The whole place seemed alive and listening ; if it were
determined to inflict upon me the sense of being an
intruder, it was certainly succeeding. But — what was
that ? The creatures, the very plants are listening to
me here — no less. I catch sight of a rabbit sitting up
with ear cocked a few feet away ; it comes with a shock
to realise that all unawares one is being watched. How
many eyes, of what creatures, are there watching me
from all round in this thicket ? Returning baffled from
various sallies to the edge of the enclosure, the thought
itself makes me a trifle cold. Or was it a cloud passing
across the sun ? Certainly an impression of grey coldness
passing over quickened the feeling of alienation : the
frightened watchfulness of the heath changed for a second
into a lowering hostility which made me anxious to find
the way out. Going forward to the stone barrier, the sun
shone bravely out and I suddenly remembered all I had
ever been told of snakes in the snake-frequented granite
parish of Luxulyan ; I thought of the kindly old men who
warned me as a boy walking here not to climb the stone
hedges. On my way forward, a bird suddenly started up
at my feet, with an immense whirring of wings : nothing
more startling ! Five rooks came clattering out of the

wilderness and over my head ; a sinister wind awoke and rustled among the leaves upon the trees in the dark lower corner of the heath. With a sudden unaccountable impulse I rushed back from my last attempt to find the way out through the hedge ; and in full career across the heath was tripped up — nothing is apt to be more tenacious than an old gorse root well entrenched — and found myself comfortably sprawling upon a large and welcome tussock of heath.

It was not until then that, the spirit appeased, the place relented towards me. At once I found the tension vanished. Turning over upon my back, I was in a position to appreciate the sky. Never a more perfect evening sky : the white clouds placid like folded sheep, hardly moving, very high up the scattered fleeces of the most distant, fine-spun clouds ; upon the hills around were the patterns of their slowly-moving shadows, blue in the distance ; in a nearer field higher up in the hills, sheep were peacefully browsing. Here in the enclosure, the rabbits were no longer afraid : they came out of hiding and went on with their cropping ; the sun came out upon the leaves of oak, ash, and syca-more and played a pretty game with the breeze, turning the undersides of the leaves to gleaming silver pennies. All the heath was rustling with friendly life. I found that my mind, no longer agitated with the problem of finding a way out, was only concerned with bringing to the surface a once-known half-guessed name : the name of a farm. A whisper seemed to come up from the withies of the wilderness, bearing a name which strangely I had had in my mind for days before finding myself there : " Is it Restinnes ? Is it Restinnes ? " it said.

" Restinnes ? Restinnes ? " it echoed in the contented chambers of my mind.

CORNISH CONVERSATION PIECE

READERS of Katherine Mansfield's *Journal* will remember how she was consoled during an illness at Looe by the wise and comforting words of Mrs. Honey. I was fortunate enough myself to be consoled during a long convalescence from illness a year or two ago by the ministrations of two old Cornishwomen, Mrs. Rosevear and her " general ", Miss Menadue. Their conversation — and my having, like Byron's angels, " little else to do " — revived an interest in the Cornish dialect which had tended to lapse with so many years away from home. I jot down these few notes as an aid to visitors intending to come to Cornwall, in case they would like to have some clue to what the Cornish are saying : they sometimes complain that it is impossible to understand them.

First, it is important to master the use of the simile, to collect as many as you can and to use them on every possible occasion. Cornish people feel some deep-rooted psychological dissatisfaction in using an adjective, to describe something, without a comparison beyond. They feel that there is something wanting to the rhythm of the sentence ; you can no more stop them (supposing you were foolish enough to want to) going on to the inevitable comparison than you can stop a cow lowing for its calf. The simile is more or less inevitable ; it is fixed and conventional. It is a mistake to ascribe the vividness of their phrases to any originality of mind, or gift of language, on the part of those who use them. You might as well give credit to the wasp or the butterfly for the vividness of their colours. In fact these phrases — and many of them are striking, some beautiful — have come down from generation to generation, from parents to children. So that when you hear something that strikes you from the lips of Mrs. Rosevear or Miss Menadue, it springs from no originality on their part, but from their mothers, and their mothers' mothers. Their speech is a folk-creation, not their own. As Swift shows so brilliantly, and with such contempt, in his instructions for *Polite Conversation*, the talk of the ordinary human fool consists almost entirely of clichés. They are none the less clichés because they are concrete and vivid with simple country people like the Cornish, than when they are faded and abstract, worn-out counters of conversation with the middle classes.

The Cornish, then, attach to the common adjectives, particularly those of physical description, an invariable simile — or perhaps there is a choice of two or three, one of which must appear. Take the word " thin ", frequently applied to me after my illness. " You'm so thin as a raake ", Mrs. Rosevear would say ; " You'm lookin' so thin as a craane (crane) ", according to Miss Menadue. " Black " may be followed by two or three similes with different shades of meaning and to suit different circumstances. If you happen to get well sunburned (a feat rather difficult in Cornwall that year), then you're " burnt so black as a craw " ; if you are annoyed and obviously feeling ill-tempered you may be " lookin' so black as sin ", or alternatively " so black as Saatan ". The sky when overcast usually looks " black as thunder ", though I have heard it referred to more personally as " black as sin ". And so on through all the adjectives of simple, personal description : " blue as a' adder " — you can also be blue, on coming in from a bathe, for example, " as a winnard ", or " lookin' like a dyin' winnard ", *i.e.* some sort of bird, I have been told lately a redwing. " Red as fire ", of course — that follows ; also " 'ot as fire " and " vex as fire ". " Sour as vinegar " is equally obvious, but also " sour as grab ", *i.e.* a crab-apple. ' Aw, my dear life, this is so sour as grab ", you might say of the stewed fruit at lunch, and you would be coming on. " Sweet ", on the other hand, offers a difficulty ; " 'tis so sweet as malotta ", is a regular phrase ; do they mean " molasses " ? One might go on almost indefinitely : " green as a lick ", *i.e.* leek ; " old as Adam " or " old as Methuselah ", of course. But what is interesting is that these last are used of smell even more frequently than of age purely and simply. " The place is smellin' so old as Adam ", they say of a dank room ; or *mutatis mutandis* of anything gone mouldy. Shades of difference in meaning, too, are indicated naturally by the simile that follows the adjectives. " Maaze as a sheep ", for instance, means stupid as a sheep ; while " maaze as a curlie " means wild as a curlew.

These are but examples of phrases ; but there are often whole sentences, too, expressing a comparison. " Aw, 'er faace is like two plaates clapped together ", a favourite way of commenting on somebody's thinness. Mrs. Rosevear's old mother, Granny V., used to say, " I've often come 'ome from town loaded like a bee ". Mrs. Rosevear always says of the beach below the cottage, when crowded with people : " They'm like a swerm o' bees there."

It will be noticed that the Cornish, like the older county gentry, are apt to drop the terminal *g*, perfectly naturally, in such words as " ridin', shootin', fishin' " — they don't do much " 'untin' " ; and, like Walter Savage Landor and Bishop Ullathorne, they are innocent of an *h*. (" I was a bishop with the mitre on me 'ead, while 'e was still a bloomin' 'eretic " : Bishop Ullathorne on Cardinal Manning.) Also it is usually *de rigueur* to use a singular verb with a plural subject, and, where possible, a verb in the plural with a singular subject. For example, " Me legs is aachin' awful " ; but — " Me 'ead do aache awful ".

The verb " to be " is in a dreadful muddle in Cornish

dialect ; the poor thing would hardly recognise itself. The present tense looks something like this :

I be	We'm, or We be
You'm (= am) ; occasionally, You be	
'Ee or she be	They be ; *but* — things is.

Personal pronouns are in a similar state of confusion — or rather the confusion is greatest where the old regularity has broken down. For example, " I said to 'ee, an' 'ee said to she " — but this form is becoming contaminated with ideas of grammatical correctness penetrating through from the elementary school. You may now hear Cornish people say " I said to him " (or more frequently " to'n ") " and 'ee said to she " ; or *vice versa*, and with variations. And also " They said to we " ; on the other hand, though this is becoming rare, " us'll " for " we will " ; for example, " Us'll tell'n what to do ".

With these few simple indications and rules, we might turn to some actual examples of conversation.

Miss Menadue is a solid, very solid, specimen of Nonconformity ; and her natural bent is to turn the conversation into moral channels. She finds the paragraph or even the sentence unsatisfying, incomplete, unless it ends with a moral. Mrs Rosevear is a child of nature ; her phrases are actually more vivid, more concrete ; she is of a more practical turn of mind : no pulling wool over the eyes of Mrs. Rosevear, a very common-sense old lady.

Here is a scrap of overheard conversation in the kitchen :

Miss M. (on her knees among the cinders, cleaning the stove) : Raachel, Raachel, weeping for her children.

Mrs. R. (caught out for once by natural curiosity) : Aw, w'at 'appened to 'em then ? I just about forget. (In fact, she never knew.)

Miss M. (who knows her Bible, if nothing else) : She wept because they were not.

Mrs. R. (annoyed at self-pity in anybody else) : W'at rot !

Miss M. (on her Nonconformist high horse) : Well, it's the Bible. Tha's what we got to go by. Tha's what governs the world. Tha's what we must follow, if we want a Christian England, etc. etc.

For all her reading the Bible by the light of a candle when she goes to bed, Miss Menadue has yet to learn a thing or two, as the following discussion shows :

Miss M. (helping old Mrs. R. to dress in the morning) : Adam and Eve sinned.

Mrs. R. (very knowing) : Dun't 'ee knaw what they done ?

Miss M. : No. They picked the fruit off the forbidden tree.

Mrs. R. (insistently) : Do 'ee knaw what their sin was ?

Miss M. (innocently) : No.

Mrs. R. : Their sin was they knawed they was naaked an' went together.

Miss M. : I dun't believe it. Their sin was that they eat the forbidden fruit, th' apple.

Mrs. R. (with the superior knowledge of experience) : Well, tha's what their sin was.

Miss M. (rather uncertain for once and surprisingly tolerant) : That idn' no sin.

Mrs. R. (who knows) : Yes, 'tis.

Miss M. (giving ground) : Well, if they was told not to sin they should 'ave knawed 'nough not to. (On her moral high horse, going out of the door.) We'm told we must knaw the good from the bad.

One thing Mrs. Rosevear and Miss Menadue are agreed upon, in deploring and decrying the disgraceful modernity of women's clothes :

Miss M. (coming home from town with the news) :
Well, I never : I saw a young woman down the town, an'
she 'ad on shorts showin' the best part of 'er leg up to 'er
thighs. A disgraace to our raace, I call it. I should be
shaamed to go round like it ; though I've got a good
shaape leg. (She is enormous : that goes without saying.) At least, so I've been told. I don't say so meself.

When I ask what a disgrace to our *race* means, Mrs.
R. explains : A disgraace to our *sec*.

Miss M. : Yes, to our sec. (A little uncertain whether
the word isn't " sect " : that sounds somehow more
familiar.)

A great thunder-storm one night that summer provided
a fine opportunity. Miss Menadue behaved like the perfect
spinster, very frightened ; lit the candle in her room, then
came into Mrs. Rosevear's bedroom for company. I
caught sight of her in the candlelight sitting on the bed
with a blanket huddled round her.

" Isn't it lovely ? " I say, on my way down to sit in the
large bay window, a first-class seat in the stalls, while the
lightning plays over the sand dunes, lights up the cliffs and
the sea.

" No, sad, very *sad*, I call it," says Miss Menadue. It
seems an odd word to use. I think of the French use of
" *triste* " — the same sense. What she wants is to moralise
on the weather. " Very sad weather," she says lachry-
mosely.

In the morning, a grand topic for conversation, a
serious and solemn face. " Very *sad* weather, I call it."

Me : Why, Miss M. ?

Miss M. : Well, you dunnaw what might 'appen. I'm
thankful to be spared.

Me : It was a lovely spectacle : Nature's handiworks.

Miss M. : Nothin' to do with Naature ; 'tes God's
'andiwork. (Then) I caan't see nothin' to laff at ; 'tes
too serious.

Me (hopefully) : Thought 'twas the end of the world, Miss M. ?

Miss M. : Well, if 'twas, I should fall to prayin' right away.

What a world of mystery and nonsense she inhabits ! But it is the world we all inhabited fifty years ago. And they say that in the far west of Cornwall there were people who were convinced that the end of the world had come that night and went round knocking each other up.

Mrs. Rosevear's version of the storm was much more practical and vivid :

" I got op to maak a drop o' water, and the lightnin' was waavin' and waavin' every minute." (It exactly describes it.) " And the thunder was roarin' miles an' miles away. Like blastin' in the quarries, g'eat rocks fallin' down."

There are, too, as you would expect, a great many local references in their conversation. If a house or a room is untidy it is said to be " like Lanson Gaol " ; or if it is not like Launceston Gaol, then it is like " Troy Town " or " Lobb's eyes ". The interesting thing is that it must be more than a century since the county gaol was transferred from Launceston to Bodmin ; yet the old phrase survives. The gaol at Launceston Castle had a bad name in former centuries for its filth and insalubriousness. The " Troy Town " referred to must be the original Troy, I think — certainly not Q.'s Troy Town. And who Lobb was, about whose eyes the Cornish are still so uncomplimentary, I have no idea. Nor who was Lady Fan (or Van) Todd, if she ever existed, who is referred to in the saying, of an overdressed woman, " See she there ! She's like Laady Fan Todd, dressed to death and killed with fashion."

HOW DICK STEPHENS FOUGHT
THE BEAR

HAVE you never heard how Dick Stephens fought the
bear ? In its time people knew that story from
Penzance to Plymouth, and the old men know it
still. But alas, not the young ones. My father knew it, and
held Dick in great account for it : as indeed he should,
for Dick was a splendid fellow. Besides which he was a
connection of our family. My father had told me before
to get Dick one day to tell me the story. And last night
at Trenarren I met him coming home from market, and
he "up and told" me, as we say. I write it down for
the benefit of posterity ; if I don't, the story will perish,
when Dick and his generation dies out, and the young
people ought to know the prowess of their fathers.

But I wish I could give you some idea of the action,
the vigour of gesture and speech of the old man. He had
been very ill with bronchitis some four years ago and it
had aged him. He was now in his seventy-fourth year he
told me, after a little preliminary bantering, like a woman,
about his age.

" 'Ow old shud 'ee think ? "

" Sixty-two," I said politely ; and it was true, he
looked a man still in his sixties.

" Se'mty-four nex' birthday," he said with an air of
triumph.

" How long ago was it since you fought the bear ? "
I said, putting the leading question at once. He had
never told me the story before, and somehow I thought
this evening he might. There was nobody about : a
beautiful July evening after rain — I had been watching
the shades of colour on fold upon fold of the land going all
the way up to Brown Willy and Rowtor, Kit Hill and the

tors of Dartmoor on the sky-line; an unnaturally pro-
longed amphitheatre of coast-line, so clear was the evening,
running all the way from Chapel Point beyond Mevagissey
to the Gribbin in the foreground, then to Rame Head
and beyond Plymouth to Start Point — a good fifty miles
— a world of coves, shingle beaches, dappled cliffs, and
deep evening-blue water.

There in the lane was Dick, the farmer of Trevissick,
before me, his arms shrunken, neck shrivelled, and a good
bit bent; but still standing over six feet in his socks and
his eye bright though a little sunken. The bell at Penrice
sounded mellow and clear out over the rook-laden woods
and the deer-park. I thought he might be willing to tell
me, but I had no idea what a performance it would be —
one in a thousand. To make sure, I told him father had
always told me to get him to tell me the story, but had
never told me himself.

" Well, — it must 'a been fifty-one or fifty-two year
ago. I was a young chap, twenty-two, I remember — I
mind as if it was yesterday. 'Twas one evenin' after work,
and I walked into town in nothin' but me shirt-sleeves
and old clothes — I thought nothin' of walkin' in to town.
There was a fair down to Fair Park, an' crowds of people.
An' there was a wrastlin' saloon with a notice op an' two
chaps — Guest they was called, from South Wales:
' 'Oo would wrastle the bear?' 'Ee was proper trained
for it you knaw. They 'ad a leather aapern, a g'eat
blacksmith's aapern for 'ee to put on to protect 'ee from
the bear's claws: rolled up 'ee was. An' 'twas, ' 'Oo wud
fight the bear? 'Oo wud wrastle the bear?' Nobody
wud come forward. I went down with y'r uncle Bill —
reglar sportin' man 'ee was: anythin' for a bit o' sport.
An' 'ee said, ' Damn 'ee, Dick, go in and fight the beggar
— that was 'ow 'ee used to talk. Well — I was a bit
bashful and never one for pushin' meself forward. An'
when they said ' 'Oo'll fight the bear?' your uncle said

' 'Ere, mister, I've got a man that'll wrastle your bear.'
So after that I 'ad to, like. So I said to'n, ' Darn 'ee, then,
I will.' An' 'ee op an' 'eaved out the aapern — 'ee was all
rolled up — out over th'eads of the crowd. When they
'eard that somebody was goin' to wrastle the bear, they
come in in 'underds.

" You knaw what a boxin' saloon is like. Well —
'twas like that. But aw — I forgot — before I took on
there was a chap called Bob Saunders — live in town now,
'ee was a maason's labourer or else a maason, g'eat big
fellow 'ee was — aw fine fellow, g'eat arms on'n : *'ee* was
goin' to fight the bear first. So we went in, and all the
people come pushin' in — the plaace was crammed : I
never saw nothin' like et. An' they 'ad a few rouns of
boxin' and wrastlin', you knaw, like they do ; and then
Bob Saunders' turn come.

" 'Ee was the sort of chap that drink a lot, went round
to pubs and anybody that was drunk 'ee'd op and giv'n
a blaw an' knock'n out. That was the sort of chap 'ee
was. Mind you a fine-built fella — aw — g'eat arms
on'n. Well — 'ee took his plaace in one corner and the
bear in th' other. G'eat brown bear 'ee was, four 'underd
poun' weight. When they said ' Time ', 'ee rawse up
from 'is corner on 'is 'ind legs and come forward — 'ee
was trained to et. My God, Bob Saunders didn' stop to
meet'n 'alf way : 'ee no sooner seed'n rise op on 'is 'ind
legs th'n 'ee give one lep and lepped right out over the rope
in among the people.

" You should 'ave seed the people laugh. Laugh ?
Bob Saunders never 'eard th'end of it for months and
months. People'd ask'n, ' 'Ow did 'ee fight the bear
then, Bob ? Deffer'nt thing to knockin' out drunk men
in pubs, wudn' it ? '

" Well, that put the wind up me a bit, I can tell 'ee.
But I didn' say nothin'. They 'ad a few more roun's of
boxin', you knaw like they do, and then my turn come.

They put up the leather aapern on me, an' then before we begin, the man said, ' There's two things I want for 'ee to understand, young man. This 'ere bear is muzzled. If you touch the muzzle 'ee'll bite your 'ead off. And the second thing is, you take'n on at your own risk ; we wun't be responsible fur anythin' that 'appens.'

" Well — they said that to put 'ee off a bit. 'N I was a braave bit frightened, but I didn' say nothin'. Well, they said ' Time ', and the bear got op from his corner, roase op on 'is 'ind legs and come forward. Mind you, I thought 'underds o' things. 'Ee come for to meet me and put out his g'eat arms an' we met. An' 'ee 'oogged me and I 'oogged 'ee. I cudn' shif'n. I tried to lift'n off his feet. But 'twas impossible. He was that weight, four 'underd pound. 'Ee was that firm——"

" Firm as a rock," I put in.

" Ess, as a rock," he repeated with emphasis and a sense of rightness. " I tried'n this way, and I tried'n that way, and I cudn' move'n. I tried to give'n a cant, an' tilt'n over. I kicked at his leg, but 'ee wudn' let go. What was I to do with'n ? I thought an' I thought : I 'ad 'old ov'm an' I didn' let'n go. An' 'ee was clever, trained to et. I noticed that 'ee was always trying to keep me op nuzzlin' under me chin and pushin' me op. An' once 'ee got one of 'is g'eat long arms right over me shoulder, and th'other under th'other. I thought me back was goin' to crack. But 'ee didn'.

" Then I thought that's 'is game, to keep me op. After that I kep'n down there, like that. I noticed 'ee was doin' all 'is work with his forearms ; an' I thought if I can get 'old of 'is arms an' pinch they, 'ee wun't be able to do so much. So I got a 'old of 'is arms, an' I pinched 'em an' pinched 'em, an' I didn' let go. I was sweatin' like a bull, and I could feel 'ee pantin' an' strugglin'. An' I thought, Now, mister, I've got 'ee. An' sure 'nough I 'ad. I 'eld on and went on pinchin'n like this——"

Here it was necessary to give me a demonstration. Farmer Dick threw down his raincoat on the grass by the roadside under the bush of honeysuckle, threw down his fairings and his stick ; I threw my walking-stick down and had my arms clinched together.

" Tha's 'ow I held'n. I cud feel 'is breath comin' an' goin'. When the people saw I 'ad'n, they was shoutin' out, ' Give it to'n, Dick. You've got'n. 'Old on, ole man. You'll do'n.' And then I 'eaved'n op sideways and give'n a twist, and thrawd'n right over on 'is back.

" You should 'ave 'eard the cheerin'. You knaw what tes like — some kick-op. They said you cud 'ear the cheerin' op town.

" The fellow that run the shaw — 'ee was a decent sort of chap, 'ee said, ' Well, tha's the first time that I've been served that trick, young man. 'Underds of people 'ave tried to thraw'n, but nobody yet 'ave been aable to do et.' Then 'ee said, ' Would 'ee tackle'n again ? '

" Well, now me blood was op, an' I felt confident like I cud thraw'n ; 'n I said, ' Ess, I'll tackle'n and thraw'n again.'

" An' all the people cheered, an' said, ' Good ole Dick, you'll thraw'n. Try'n again.' An' I did. There 'ee was back in 'is corner pantin', an' I was sweatin' like wan thing.

" Well, w'en they said ' Time ', 'ee come for me. 'Ee was angry, min' you : never been thraw'd like that before. 'Ee come at me, and got 'is fore-paw roun' the back of me 'ead : 'ee give me a blaw, drawd blood, made me smart, I can tell 'ee. I got the mark, a little mark, there now."

We stopped to inspect the place, which I must confess, after half a century, in the fading light was indecipherable.

" But this time I knew 'ow to thraw'n, an' it didn' take me long. But before I thraw'd'n, he op with 'is 'ind leg, and give me such a blaw in the guts — my God, it made me feel sick, fit to spew, for a minute. But I got 'is arms pinched and it didn' taake me long this time, I give'd'n a cant and 'eave'n right over, a'most out into where the people was.

" You shud 'ave 'eard the cheerin'. Aw, my dear life, there was some kick-op. I can mind it now, and all the people comin' op town was tellin' 'bout it, 'ow Dick Stephens thraw'd the bear. I didn' knaw et at the time, but et seems between the first an' secon' roun' father was in town, and people said to'n, 'Your boy is down there goin' to wrastle the bear,' and 'ee come in and saw the second roun'. I didn' knaw then. But afterwards——

" Aw, I forgot to tell 'ee. I 'ad me shirt-sleeves op ; and w'en we was swayin' to and fro, the bear got 'is nawse op and through his muzzle with a twick, 'ee twicked me sleeve right off be the 'em. So in th' interval, 'ee falled down on me 'an', an' I put'n in me pocket.

" W'en I got 'ome that 'evenin', mother was in the kitchen — I can mind et as if 'twas yesterday ; good mother she was to me an' a mother to everybody — I come in an' I sit down in the chair. An' I said, ' 'Ere, mother, 'ere's me sleeve for 'ee to mend.'

" She said, 'All right, boy. Ow did 'ee come to tear'n like that ? '

" So I said, ' 'Aw, I've been in town fightin' the bear.'

" With that father come in and 'ee op and told the story. An' all she said was, ' You ought to 'ave a box on the side of your ear.' Wonderful mother she was to we. An' tha's about all was said about it."

The story had come to an end. It had been told with a wealth of action : the old man had put himself into it for me : he was re-living the experience that was the high-water mark of his life. His fine dark eyes flashed ; strength came back into the shrunken arms. Once we had to scuttle into the hedge for a passing car ; still the story went on. Now it was finished.

Farmer Dick has a splendid, broad-shouldered son, as strong as his father, in the Metropolitan Police. As a postscript, he added : " W'en I was op to London with George an' we went to the Zoo, we saw a big brown bear. An' I said to'n, ' There's a bear, George, like the one I fought in town that time.' People d'knaw that story from Penzance to Plymouth."

The sun was going down behind the woods of Penrice, as the sun was going down, gently, evenly, hardly perceptibly, for him. The mellow notes of the bell struck ten. It was time to part and go home our respective ways.

" Yes," he said, " it must 'ave been fifty-one or fifty-two year ago." And a dark shadow, the shadow of time, came into his eyes.

PAGEAT OF PLYMOUTH [1]

NARRATOR. Today is the 500th anniversary of the granting of Plymouth's Charter by King Henry VI, November 12th, 1439. A great deal of water has flown down the Tamar and out into Plymouth Sound since then. Plymouth's Charter, incorporating it as a borough, granting the town self-government under its own Mayor, was granted by the King in Parliament, not simply by Royal Charter as with practically all other boroughs. In that curious fact Plymouth is very exceptional : it took an Act of Parliament to make Plymouth a borough. You will hear the story tonight of how it was done.

CHANTER. Wherever you are, turn your minds to that lovely city in the far west, sitting throned upon her seven hills, half-girdled with the waters of the Hamoaze, of Tamar and Tavy and Plym, with Cattewater and Millbay and Sutton Pool, that town looking out from her fortress across the waters of the Sound, out to sea, keeping watch and ward at the western entrance to the Channel as through the centuries that have gone, the gateway to America and the Seven Seas.

WOMAN'S VOICE. Think of what Plymouth looks like to an exile returning home to England after many years. The great liner slips softly into the Sound between Cawsand and the Breakwater ; on one side the grey cliffs of Cornwall, on the other the red cliffs of Devon. And there before you, in the early haze of the morning, is the town, tier upon tier of houses rising from those sea-lapped walls, the Hoe, the Citadel, Saltash Bridge, the

[1] Draft of broadcast commemorating the Quincentenary of Plymouth's Charter, November 12th, 1939.

green heights of Dartmoor.   After long years of voyaging it is pleasant to return.

Think of Plymouth as I saw it one early morning in June this summer from the heights of the Hoe.   It wasn't long after dawn ; there was the sun in the east making a silver mirror of Cattewater ; the blinds of the houses upon the Hoe were still drawn ; nobody was abroad ; hardly anything was stirring : a few sparrows were chittering around the houses, the sea-birds were still asleep.   Out there upon the water, all the innumerable little white boats were anchored, like seagulls, holding themselves so still, in a trance waiting for day with its myriad activities and labours of a great city to begin.

WOMAN (*singing the refrain of the old carol*) :

O dear Plymouth town, and O blue Plymouth Sound !
O where is your equal on earth to be found ?

CHANTER.   Think of the thousand various sounds of a city waking to life, the milk-cart rattling over the paving stones, the postman's van, the knock at the door, the newspaper boy, the noises of the streets beginning.   But towns have their characteristic sounds, particularly a great port like Plymouth, with liners entering and leaving the Sound, the shrill whistle of the tugs, the roar of the sea-planes rising from Cattewater, the chaffer of the fish-women down on the Barbican, the whistle of the engines steaming out of North Road Station, the clamour of the dockyard at Devonport, the bugles from the Citadel upon the Hoe.   Above all, there is the sound of the sea to whose rhythms and tides Plymouth life has rocked through all the ages ; the bells of St. Andrew's to call to mind all that past, all those memories of the generations that have gone, to keep us true to the history we share with them.

Fade away sounds — bells last of all.

NARRATOR (*in a prose voice*).   Actually, Plymouth is not so very old as towns go : nothing like so old as Exeter which goes right back to Roman times, or Barnstaple which celebrated its thousandth anniversary as a corporate town a few years ago. You've heard the old rhyme—

> Plympton was a borough town
> When Plymouth was a fuzzy down.

I *have* heard people say *Saltash* was a borough town, etc., but they must have been Cornish people, perhaps Saltash people themselves. And in the old days, in the reign of Queen Elizabeth, there was no love lost between Saltash and Plymouth. So far as Cornish people are concerned, there has always been a feeling, half of rivalry, half pride, in watching Plymouth's rise to fortune and glory.

PLYMOUTH MAN. Yu wouldn' say they haven' ben pleased to share in the good fortune, now, would yu ?

CORNISHMAN. No, there you 'ave me right nuff. But all the saame, we Cornish volks 'ave done a good deal to lay the foundaations like. We'm always glad to see the young ones comin' along and doin' well — per'aps better'n might 'ave been expected ef twadn' for we.

NARRATOR. Now no quarrelling, you two. The fact is that all through Plymouth's history there has been a considerable Cornish contribution : Trelawnys, Tresawles, Edgecumbes, Grenvilles, Footes.

PLYMOUTH MAN. Yu'll be tellin' us Sir Francis Drake was a Cornishman next.

CORNISHMAN. Well, he wudn'. But 'ee did the next best thing to put it right be marryin' a girl from our side the Tamar, didn' a ?

NARRATOR. So you say. You can see the entry in the register at St. Budeaux church up on its hill there looking out over the river towards Cornwall to this day. There now, you can hear the bells of St. Budeaux, rather faint and far away, if you listen — but sweet all the same, as on that summer's day 370 years ago, when the young captain, Francis Drake, married his bride Mary Newman.

It wasn't long after he came home from that famous third voyage of John Hawkins, which met with disaster, when the Spaniards attacked them without warning in harbour at San Juan de Ulloa with overwhelming numbers, and they had to fly home across the Atlantic, battered, the expedition ruined, starving, the men dying like flies on board. Drake never forgot ; he vowed vengeance, and lived to see another day. It's touching, don't you think, to see that little entry in the old parchment book after so many years :

4th July, 1569 : Francis Drake and Mary Newman

Bells distant.

Now . . .

CHANTER :

Drake he's in his hammock an' a thousand mile away,
(Capten, art tha sleepin' there below ?)
Slung atween the round shot in Nombre Dios Bay,
An' dreamin' arl the time o' Plymouth Hoe.
Yarnder lumes the Island, yarnder lie the ships,
Wi' sailor-lads a-dancin' heel-an'-toe,
An' the shore-lights flashin', an' the night-tide dashin',
He sees et arl so plainly as he saw et long ago.

Slight tremor of drum.

NARRATOR. Nevertheless, in spite of the comparative lateness of Plymouth in attaining its majority, winning its charter of incorporation and becoming a borough with mayor and aldermen and council, with maces and staves and what not, West-Country people have always believed in the story of a mythical settlement here right back beyond history. The story begins with a wrestling match upon Plymouth Hoe between Corinaeus and the giant Gogmagog for the possession of the country. The delightful Elizabethan writer, Richard Carew of Antony, from across the water, his house looking down upon the St. Germans river, tells us . . .

READER (*turning the pages of Carew's " Survey of Cornwall ", 1602*). " Corinaeus, cousin to Brutus, the first conqueror of this Island : who wrastling at Plymouth (as they say) with a mighty giant called Gogmagog threw him over cliff, brake his neck and received the gift of that country, in reward for his prowess."

NARRATOR (*breaking in*). But Carew was a Cornishman, and therefore, you may think, too imaginative. However that may be, the curious thing is . . .

READER. Let me go on in Carew's own words . . . (*Rustling the pages, finding the place.*) " Moreover upon the Hawe at Plymouth there is cut in the ground the portraiture of two men, the one bigger, the other lesser, with clubbes in their hands (whom they term Gog Magog), and (as I have learned) it is renewed by order of the townesmen when cause requireth, which should inferr the same to be a monument of some moment."

NARRATOR. . . . the curious thing is that I've seen this borne out in the old records of the town, kept in the archives beneath the Guildhall ; from time to time they would renew these figures cut out in the turf upon the Hoe. In 1514, for example : " John Lucas, Sergeant, had 8d. for cutting Gogmagog " ; in 1567, 20d. was spent upon " new cutting the Gogmagog ". It must have been a landmark as recognisable as the Giant carved upon the hill above Cerne Abbas, or the White Horse that you see from the train at Westbury. It was destroyed when they built the Citadel in good King Charles' golden days.

PLYMOUTH MAN. Ah, there yu be again. Yu never did see such a place as Plymouth is for pullin' down and destroyin' interestin' things. There's the Corporation 've been and allowed the Theatre Royal tu be destroyed this very year.

NARRATOR. The pity of it ! Yes, you're right ; a peculiar fatality seems to have hung over the old historic buildings of Plymouth. Plymouth seems to have made away with more memorials of its historic past than most towns accumulate in their history. Hardly anything remains of the Castle, nothing of the lovely old Hoe gates, or of the walls that surrounded the town ; nothing of the Friary, nothing of Palace Court, where the Priors of Plympton had their place ; nothing of the wealthy merchants' houses where Drake and the Hawkinses lived ; nothing of the great architect Foulston's Royal Union Baths, as fine as anything at Regency Brighton. All pulled down in the nineteenth century ; and now they are destroying the magnificent group of his Theatre Royal and Royal Hotel, the gem of Plymouth's architecture, the *clou* of the whole lay-out of the town.

READER. Ah, well ! It's pleasanter to think of the old times.

NARRATOR. Certainly you will find that Plymouth men kept up their interest in wrestling all through the centuries : there are payments in the town's accounts to wrestlers, as well as for shooting at the butts upon the Hoe, to the players and morris dancers that entertained the good citizens long ago . . .

Snatch from a morris dance, accompanied by a tambourine.

PLYMOUTH MAN. Yu've heard, maybe, of the game of bowls, now ? D'yu find anything in those old records to prove to us whether they really played bowls in those days or no ? We believe that there was a game of bowls played once, yu know, up on the Hoe . . .

NARRATOR. If we listen carefully, we may hear something of that game, hear the woods knocking against each other, hitting the jack.

Clatter of wooden clogs coming up the alley to the bowling green.

MESSENGER. Sir Francis, your worships, there's a pinnace just come round Penlee with the news that the Spaniards are off the Lizard.

81

BABBLE OF VOICES.
{ We must stop the game !
No time to finish now.
We must make speed aboard.
Away, away.

DRAKE. How many sail, do they say ?

MESSENGER. More than a hundred, Sir Francis.

DRAKE. The Lord be praised who has brought us to this day. The God of battles, He will see us through. I trust we shall give such good account of ourselves that the Duke of Medina Sidonia will wish himself ere long at St. Mary Port among his orange trees.

LORD HOWARD. We leave our game, Sir Francis, for a greater and more perilous.

DRAKE. My lord, you shall not escape so easily. There's time to finish this game, and to thrash the Spaniards too.

He bowls his wood, there is a resounding smack as Drake's wood knocks Howard's away and takes the jack.

CHANTER :

Take my drum to England, hang et by the shore,
  Strike et when your powder's runnin' low ;
If the Dons sight Devon, I'll quit the port o' Heaven,
  An' drum them up the Channel as we drummed them
    long ago.
    Drum.

NARRATOR. The ancient game of bowls has never ceased to have its attraction for West Countrymen, from that day to this, though the day has gone when every little inn had its bowling alley in the garden at the back. However, there are signs that the game is coming back into its own again. I am glad that they still play bowls on Plymouth Hoe.

But the West-Country sport of wrestling isn't what it was, I'm sorry to say. All Devon and Cornish men have heard of the famous encounter between Polkinghorne and Abraham Cann at Plymouth a hundred years ago. The match took place on Tamar Green at Devonport,

October 23rd, 1826. There were 17,000 spectators to see it. Polkinghorne was the Cornish champion, a huge fellow, landlord of the " Red Lion " at St. Columb. Cann was the Devonshire champion, a smaller man, closer knit and more scientific. Polkinghorne had already thrown several Devonshire men, and when Cann met him, to rectify the disparity, he wore a pair of shoes whose toes had been baked into flint. Polkinghorne was in his stockings, and took a terrible punishing from Cann's kicks. It was a terrific contest, which lasted ten rounds. They each threw the other once ; when Polkinghorne threw Cann again and it was disallowed, he left the ring and Cann was awarded the stakes by default.

It was a heroic battle, the memory of which has been handed down from generation to generation in the West Country. But no Devon or Cornish man ever felt satisfied with the result.

READER. The place that wrestling used to have with us is now taken by football, and both counties take pride in the exploits of Plymouth Argyle. Plymouth draws the two together. On a Saturday afternoon in the season, when Plymouth Argyle is playing some big League match at home, thousands of Cornishmen go up by rail and bus and car and bike, flocking into Home Park for the match. Now you can hear them . . .

Noise of crowd at football match. Shouts of " Go on, Vidler," " Well played, Black," etc. " Get on with it," " Put some ginger into it," and so on.

CHANTER. Cast your mind back from the great and busy city of today, with its industry, the hive of many activities, its populousness, the Plymouth of the Three Towns — to the first steps of that small community of fisher-folk down by the water-side. Life was hard and dangerous in those days, exposed to all the weathers and to innumerable enemies.

READER. Almost the first we hear of Tamarside is an

entry in the Anglo-Saxon Chronicle of a raid made by the Danes in 997. Their fleet came round Land's End on the south side, " and went then into the mouth of the Tamar and burned and destroyed therein all they met with, and they burned Ordulf's Minster at Tavistock and brought much booty with them to their ships ".

NARRATOR. In those days, a thousand years ago, there weren't more than a few houses at Sutton. And in time the little place came into the possession of the rich priory of Plympton, up the river. Under the fostering care of the monks, the little town throve, became bigger and more important. In the French wars of Edward III, Plymouth and the ports thereabouts sent 26 ships and 603 men to the siege of Calais.

READER. Carew says : " Here the never enough commended Black Prince, attended by the Earls of Warwick, Suffolk, Salisbury, and Oxford, the Lord Chandos and others, committed himself to the sea, with a navy of 300 bottoms for landing and maintaining his father's right in France ; and hither after his glorious battle at Poictiers he returned with the captive French King and his nobles ".

WOMAN'S VOICE. Many years later he came home yet again, stricken now with disease. He landed here at Plymouth with his Princess, and the little Richard their son, afterwards King. The Black Prince had come home to die.

NARRATOR. The Frenchmen rewarded Plymouth with their attentions. In 1399 they attacked the town. In 1403, the Sieur du Chastel with a fleet of Normans and Bretons made a descent upon it and set fire to a part of the town. They still call that place Briton Side. In these ways the town attained its majority, grew up and out of the leading-strings of the monks at Plympton.

CHANTER. Think of the contrast : on one side the lives of the monks, the ordered, the immemorial routine, the watches in the night, the ceaseless offering of prayer at their altars, life passing away in a dream.

Record of Gregorian chant. A bell strikes.

On the other, the secular life with its hazards and temptations, the daily work, the give and take of common life, the thrill of adventure, the courage of men, the endurance of women.

Record of sounds at the Barbican, the whipping of cords on a boat, smacking of canvas, a windlass, fish being loaded, rolling of barrels in street.

NARRATOR. The citizens tired of their leading-strings. A party grew up in the town which challenged the rights of the Lord Prior. They chose their own mayor in place of the reeve whom the Prior set over them. There were disputes between the men of Plymouth and the Prior ; judgment was given against them. The past was on the side of the monks but the future was with the townsmen. In the year 1439 they sent up a petition to the King, which said :

READER (*turning parchment*). " That the town of Sutton Prior, the tithing of Sutton Ralph, and the hamlet of Sutton Vautort, which town, tithing, and hamlet are commonly called Plymouth, are so near the coasts of the sea, and that there is so great a concourse of ships, as well of enemies as of others, in the port ; and that the town aforesaid hath often from defects in their walls been burnt and destroyed, and the inhabitants despoiled of their goods by night and by day, and many of the inhabitants taken away into foreign ports and there imprisoned. . . . Upon which premises considered it is prayed that the King, with the consent of Parliament, for the salvation of the said town and that the inhabitants of the same may dwell there more quietly and securely, do allow the said town to be enclosed and fortified. And that the King be pleased to grant that the town from henceforth be a free borough incorporate, with a mayor and commonalty, and for ever be called the borough of Plymouth."

NARRATOR. To which petition the King gave his assent in the time-honoured formula . . .

READER. Le Roi le veut. . . .

Fade words in cheering of the citizens : " Hurrah ", " God Save the King ". *Record of a* " Te Deum Laudamus " *sung in the church of St. Andrew's. The bells ringing a peal.*

NARRATOR. That was in November 1439, in the eighteenth year of our Sovereign Lord King Henry VI. There have been many wise and discreet citizens who have followed William Kethridge, the first mayor, in that office : some of them men who have played their part in the nation's story.

READER. There was William Hawkins the elder, mayor in 1532–3 and again in 1538–9. He was among the first to send out voyages to the African coast, and the first Englishman to send his ships to Brazil, bringing back ivory from the one — elephant's teeth, they wrote it down in the old customs ledgers — and Brazil wood from the other.

NARRATOR. You may have heard the story of Martin Cockeram.

PLYMOUTH MAN. No, I don't know that I have. And what did he du then ?

READER. Hakluyt tells us that on one of old William Hawkins' voyages to Brazil, one of the savage chiefs " was contented to take ship with him and to be transported hither into England ". Hawkins left Martin Cockeram of Plymouth behind as a pledge for the chief's safety. Imagine the astonishment the chief caused with his tattooed face when he appeared at the polite court of Henry VIII.

NARRATOR. Alas, on the way back to Brazil, he died at sea.

READER. " Nevertheless, the savages being fully persuaded of the honest dealing of our men with their prince,

86

restored again the said pledge, without any harm to him."

NARRATOR. And Martin lived out his full length of days, after his strange adventure in Brazil, dying an old townsman of Plymouth, well known to all.

READER. It isn't to be wondered at that old William Hawkins, according to Hakluyt, was " a man for his wisdom, value, experience, and skill in sea causes, much esteemed and valued of King Henry VIII ".

NARRATOR. From his house in Kinterbury Street he directed his affairs, built up his fortune, and brought up his family, of whom his second son, Sir John, became famous. His elder son, another William, remained at home in charge of the business. In the reign of Queen Elizabeth, out of a list of 16 big ships owned in Plymouth, 13 belonged to the Hawkinses. This second William was mayor in the great year, *annus mirabilis*, 1588.

READER. It was he who wrote the brief eloquent note to the Lords of the Council on that July day to say that " the Spanish fleet was in view of this town yester-night, and that my Lord Admiral was passed to the sea before our said view, and was out of our sight. Since which time we have certain knowledge, both by certain pinnaces come from his Lordship, as also by plain view this present morning, that my Lord being to the windwards of the enemy, are in fight, which we beheld."

CHANTER. Think of the excitement in that small, faithful town, in the hearts of the beholders upon the Hoe, upon the cliffs, watching that fascinating, that dangerous spectacle, the Armada sweeping onwards in a great crescent-moon, the many-coloured flags flying at their masts, the crusade for the conversion of England. Slowly they passed by Plymouth, pursued, harassed by the English ships, on up the Channel to Calais, into the North Sea and round the coast of Scotland, to their end upon the Outer Hebrides, upon the rocks of Ireland, only a small remnant ever reaching Spain again.

Guns. Drum.

READER. " God blew with his breath and his enemies were scattered."

NARRATOR. These were the golden days of Plymouth, the heroic age. There was always something exciting happening then, the small town pulsating with life. One day it would be the young Captain Francis returning from the voyage which first brought him fame and fortune, when he robbed the mule-trains carrying gold and silver upon the high road to Nombre de Dios in the Spanish Main, and brought his booty home safe to Plymouth.

READER. As the chronicler of that voyage tells us : " And so we arrived at Plymouth on Sunday about sermon time August 9th, 1573. At what time the news of our Captain's return brought unto his friends did so speedily pass over all the church, and surpass their minds with desire and delight to see him that very few or none remained with the preacher, all hastening to see the evidence of God's love and blessing towards our gracious Queen and country, by the fruit of our Captain's labour and success."

CHANTER. Imagine the scene in St. Andrew's church that morning : the news passing through the congregation like a breeze over a field of corn, the agitation, the excitement which can no longer be suppressed so that they all break out of church and rush helter-skelter down the hill, down Ship Street to the Barbican to welcome the fortunate Captain. You can hear their footsteps now, very faint and far away, the footsteps of men and women dead these three hundred years and more.

Record. . . .

NARRATOR. Or it is another day and the news of Drake and Hawkins' last voyage comes home to the grief-stricken town. For both captains, full of years and honours, worn out by their labours, died on that voyage and were buried at sea : Sir Francis off Portobello, not many leagues from Nombre de Dios, all his voyaging done.

READER. " Next day they carried him a league off and buried him in the sea amid lament of trumpet and roar of cannon."

CHANTER :

Drake he's in his hammock till the great Armadas come,
   (Capten, art tha sleepin' there below ?)
Slung atween the round shot, listenin' for the drum,
   An' dreamin' arl the time o' Plymouth Hoe.
Call him on the deep sea, call him up the Sound,
   Call him when ye sail to meet the foe ;
Where the old trade's plyin' an' the old flag flyin'
   They shall find him ware an' wakin' as they found him
     long ago !
   Three beats of drum softly.

NARRATOR. Those were great days indeed. The town was full of now famous men coming and going. It felt honoured by their presence, was careful to entertain them hospitably. We find many entries in the town's accounts, for sugar, wine, etc., when these gentlemen came, of dinners provided for Sir Francis and his lady, a great banquet when the Earl of Bedford or other Lords of the Council visited the town.

PLYMOUTH MAN. What *I* should like to know, is whether the cost of all this entertaining fell upon the rates ?

NARRATOR. Well, I suppose it did. But people didn't seem to complain. I suppose they felt it due to Plymouth to keep up their town's good name for hospitality. There must have been many good evenings spent, after the day's hard work, at the " Turk's Head " or the " Pope's Head " or the " Mitre ", Plymouth's famous old hostelries.

READER. We mustn't forget that it wasn't only war-time expeditions that set sail from Plymouth, but many of the most famous voyages of discovery. Carew tells us — and he knew many of these men personally — " Here

mostly have the troops of adventurers made their rendez-
vous for attempting new discoveries and inhabitancies, as
Thomas Stukely for Florida, Sir Richard Grenville for
Virginia, Sir Humphrey Gilbert for Newfoundland, Sir
Martin Frobisher and Master Davis for the North-West
Passage, Sir Walter Raleigh for Guiana ".

NARRATOR. Here Sir Walter came back from his last
fatal enterprise to find gold and found an Empire in
Guiana, to meet his death at the hands of a monarch who
was unworthy of such a subject.

CHANTER :

> Even such is Time, which takes in trust
> Our youth, our joys, and all we have,
> And pays us but with age and dust,
> Who in the dark and silent grave,
> When we have wandered all our ways,
> Shuts up the story of our days.

NARRATOR. But Plymouth men have always been
proud of his memory, as of others who have brought
honour and fame to the town.

READER. As they in turn have been proud of the place
that gave them birth. Here are the words of young Sir
Richard Hawkins, the third generation of that family who
achieved renown, saying farewell on his voyage into the
Pacific, following in the footsteps of Drake — though he
had no such good fortune, and, captured after a famous
fight, spent long years in imprisonment in Spain : " I
luffed near the shore to give my farewell to all the inhabitants of the town whereof the most part were gathered
together upon the Hoe to show their grateful correspond-
ency to the love and zeal which I, my father and pre-
decessors have ever borne to that place as to our natural
and mother town ; and first with my noise of trumpets,
after with my waits, and then with my other music, and
lastly with the artillery of my ships, I made the best

signification I could of a kind farewell. This they answered with the waits of the town and the ordnance on the shore, and with shouting of voices ; which with the fair evening and silence of the night were heard a great distance off."

Distant trumpets, music, guns.

NARRATOR. Best known of all the voyages to you, that of the *Mayflower*, which left Plymouth on " Wednesday, 6 September 1620, the wind coming east-north-east, a fine small gale ". The Pilgrim Fathers, a company of 102, men, women, and children, were leaving their native land to seek religious liberty in the New World, and found a new state on the other side of the Atlantic. In them we share a common memory with our kith and kin in America, and send our greetings to the state of Massachusetts and the new Plymouth overseas.

CHANTER. We pray Thee, Father of all men, so to guide our steps over the trackless paths of the sea, avoiding, if it be Thy will, the perils and dangers of the deep, that we may reach in Thy good time a land where we may serve Thee according to Thy will. . . .

Record of voices singing a metrical psalm.

NARRATOR. The triumphs of Plymouth have been no less in the arts of peace than in those of war. No time now to traverse all that crowded past. But we mustn't forget that Plymouth in the eighteenth century gave birth to three of the most distinguished painters of their time. Let us recall their shades : Sir Joshua Reynolds, the greatest of them. Sir Joshua, Plymouth is proud of you : you conferred an honour upon the town by being born within its boundaries.

SIR JOSHUA (*politely*). My dear sir, if you will pardon me, a slight mistake : I was born in the township of Plympton.

PLYMOUTH MAN. Never you mind about that, Sir Joshua ; going at our present rate of progress Plympton soon will be brought inside the boundaries of the Three Towns.

SIR JOSHUA. To be sure, to be sure, but a little confusing to an old gentleman whose eyesight is failing, and whose hearing isn't what it was.

CHANTER. Nevertheless, the hand retains its magic still.

SIR JOSHUA. You are very kind. Mine was a happy life ; I was happy in my art ; success came easily to me ; the cup of life was full for me.

NARRATOR. James Northcote . . .?

NORTHCOTE. Not so for me. Life was more of a struggle to the son of a watchmaker, born in Market Street. But I made good ; I made my way in London ; I painted the pictures I wanted to paint ; I fulfilled what I had it in me to do ; I had good friends ; I am content.

NARRATOR. Benjamin Haydon . . .?

HAYDON. I was unhappy ; I was never content. Some demon in my mind led me on to attempt what I could not achieve, to create the impossible. I painted great pictures ; but no one understood my genius. I was lonely ; I was poor ; I had no friends. I died by my own hand.

NARRATOR. Yet Haydon, too, left his name inscribed upon the long roll of great men, of men of genius, to whom this town gave birth, or here lived and worked and died.

READER. Divines like Zachary Mudge and Dr. Hawker of Charles Church ; the distinguished philosopher, Joseph Glanvill, whose book *The Vanity of Dogmatizing* inspired a great English poem, Matthew Arnold's ' Scholar Gipsy ' ; Arnold's contemporary, the poet Robert Stephen Hawker, the Parson of Morwenstow, was a Plymouth man born, and here, too, he died. Other and later painters lived and worked here : Samuel Prout, the water-colourist ; Sir Charles Eastlake, who when young painted Napoleon Bonaparte upon the *Bellerophon* in Plymouth Harbour ;

Edward Opie. There was William Cookworthy, who first manufactured china in England here ; and Captain Scott, sailor and explorer, born at Devonport in 1868, died in the Antarctic in 1912.

NARRATOR. Scientists, lawyers, scholars, seamen, men of business and of affairs — Plymouth has been a prolific mother of men of genius, of talent and remark.

CHANTER. In the end we think of the place that bore them all. We think of the streets that they knew, the scenes they would still recognise if they were to revisit them by the glimpse of the moon.

NARRATOR. We think of the adorable, musty atmosphere of St. Andrew's church, where so many of them were christened, where they were married and buried, where they worshipped generation after generation, all those dear shades crowding in upon us with their memories of long ago, thronging the dark aisles in the watches of the night.

Bells of St. Andrew's, very distant.

CHANTER. Night draws down upon the Hoe, upon that lovely water of the Sound, enfolds Drake's Island lying there so quietly in the silence ; upon the seaplanes like great birds at rest upon the surface of Cattewater, upon the rounded bluff of Mount Edgcumbe, upon Saltram cliffs and Cawsand. The lights come out upon the Hoe, where the footsteps have now ceased to tread and all is quiet ; lights in the myriad small craft lying at anchor, upon the Breakwater and far out to sea, the Eddystone. May God's blessing rest upon this town and all who work there ; may she ever prosper and all her sons bear themselves bravely as their fathers before them, worthy heirs of so heroic a past.

Confusion of sounds, bells, seaplanes, birds, in the end a bugle blows, three soft blows on Drake's drum.

93

THE DUCHY OF CORNWALL

RECENT events have brought the Duchy of Cornwall, or rather its revenues, very much to the fore.[1] There has been much coming and going of its officers ; never have they occupied so prominent a position in the public eye. Indeed, the public may well have wondered at this sudden importance the Duchy has attained ; it has served to call to mind the existence of a peculiarly interesting institution, with a constitutional status and characteristics all its own, of which few people are aware and with which only a few lawyers are competent to deal.

It is first necessary to clear out of the way the popular confusion between the Duchy and the county of Cornwall. They are, of course, two entirely separate entities, utterly differing in character. The one is an ordinary — or to a Cornishman, a not so very ordinary — English shire, as it might be Devonshire or Dorset ; whereas the Duchy is an institution, a great landed estate vested in the eldest son of the Sovereign (or, in the absence of a son, lying dormant in the Crown), an estate which has been based from time immemorial upon extensive lands in Cornwall, and which has existed as a duchy, save for the interregnum of the Commonwealth period, since 1337. So that we are just on the threshold of celebrating its sexcentenary.

The habit of referring to the " Duchy " when people mean the county of Cornwall is no doubt due more than anything to one of Q.'s early books, *The Delectable Duchy*, the title of which caught on and has become popularised over the last forty years — in itself a tribute to that charming volume of stories.

I remember, when my name was entered in the register

[1] Written after the Abdication of Edward VIII, in 1937.

as a Fellow of my college at Oxford, I was entered as
having been born in the " Duchy " of Cornwall. It
was intended as a compliment, and, for sentimental
reasons, taken as such, without protest. But it was in-
accurate. The popular habit of referring to Cornwall as
the " Duchy " — in the sixteenth century they called it
a " shire " like any other English shire — is a modern
error ; it may be compared to what grammarians call
the " transferred epithet ".

For all that, the Duchy, in the exact sense — the
appanage of the Duke when there is one, and when there
is not, lying dormant in the Crown — is no less interesting
and curious historically than it is on legal and constitutional grounds. For one thing, it goes back direct as an
institution to the reign of Edward III, who created it for
the support of his eldest son, the Black Prince ; and in-
directly to the Norman earldom of Cornwall, and perhaps
further than that to the conquests of the House of Wessex
upon Cornish soil. For it is worth noting that two of the
Duchy castles, Launceston and Trematon, were at places
with names ending in " ton ", indicating Saxon settlement ; and their positions guarded entries into or exits
from Cornwall across the Tamar — the one in the north,
the other in the south.

Saxon settlement does not seem to have gone a great
way further into Cornwall ; but it was a conquered
country when the Saxons themselves were conquered by
William of Normandy. He made his half-brother,
Robert of Mortain, Earl of Cornwall, who immediately
began the building of the castles at Launceston and
Trematon, the strategic keys of the county. Something
of the status of conquest remained on under the earldom
and into the Duchy. For it is significant that the lands
of both earldom and Duchy have always been concentrated in the eastern half of the county ; while villeinage
went on on the Duchy manors in Cornwall longer than

anywhere else in the country. I have myself come across in the Record Office numbers of manumissions of bond-men upon these manors right throughout the sixteenth century, in the reigns of Henry VII, Mary, and Elizabeth ; and it was not until the reign of James I that all were finally freed. The surname " Bond ", not uncommon in Cornwall, goes back to the time when they were unfree in status, villeins tied to the land, at the will of their lord — in this case the Duchy. These manumissions were made in greatest number upon the manor of Stokeclimsland, the largest of the Duchy manors, still the chief agricultural centre of the Duchy in Cornwall, in which Edward VIII as Duke always displayed a close personal interest.

Of the Norman Earls of Cornwall, the most famous and the most magnificent was Richard, King of the Romans, brother of Henry III, and the most important person in the kingdom, after the King. He was a crusader and went to Palestine in 1240. He returned to England to become a prominent figure in internal politics — his brother was having great difficulty with the popular opposition led by Simon de Montfort — and later became a personage of European importance. For he used his great wealth as Earl of Cornwall and Count of Poitou to assure himself of his election as Holy Roman Emperor. He was elected by the majority of the electors ; but, in spite of his coronation at Aix-la-Chapelle, he never could secure the obedience to his rule of more than the immediate Rhineland. Defeated by the intricacies and intrigues of German politics, when his money ran out he returned to this country and the resources of his earldom.

In the last years of his life he turned his attention to Cornwall, greatly strengthening his position there by gaining possession of Tintagel and Trematon Castles, and persuading the last of the Cardinhams to hand over Restormel Castle and the town of Lostwithiel. From this time Lostwithiel became the chief administrative centre of the earldom in Cornwall, as it subsequently remained for centuries for the Duchy. Richard's son, Edmund Earl of Cornwall, 1272–99, built between the church and the river there a fine range of buildings to house the administrative offices, which became known as the " Duchy Palace ". Here was the Shire Hall, in which the county court met, the exchequer of the earldom, later of the Duchy, the Coinage Hall (for Lostwithiel was one of the stannary towns for the coinage of tin), and the gaol for the Cornish stannaries, which continued in use as late as the eighteenth century for prisoners brought before the stannary courts. Thus on a small scale, Mr. Charles Henderson says, the Duchy Palace " represented the great Palace of Westminster now incorporated in the Houses of Parliament. Westminster had its great hall, its exchequer, its prison and government offices." The Shire Hall was a very fine thirteenth-century building which existed up to the eighteenth century, but, with that disrespect or ignorant vandalism which the Cornish people often display towards beautiful things or historical monuments of the past, was subsequently destroyed. Only a small fragment remains of the buildings which once adorned the little quayside at Lostwithiel ; you may still see something of a hall, and the remains of walls and archways built into adjacent houses indicate to the regretful visitor what once stood there.

Restormel Castle, some way out of the town, high up on a hill above the lovely valley of the Fowey, the river rippling down between the oaks and glades of fern, has been more fortunate. After an uneventful history — though it woke to life once again in the Civil War, when it was besieged and taken in turn by Parliament and the King — it has now fallen into the careful hands of the Office of Works. Stripped of devouring ivy and with walls made firm and secure, the round shell of the keep stands well up on its hill, where one may see it among the trees on the right hand as the train nears Lostwithiel.

The earldom as organised by Richard and Edmund was substantially what constituted the Duchy later. There was an intervening period after Edmund's death in 1299, when Piers Gaveston, Edward II's favourite, became earl, and after he came to his end John of Eltham, the King's second son. Upon his death Edward III decided to use the vacant earldom as a means of support for his eldest son, who had not yet been created Prince of Wales. He did so in a form to last ; for as he constituted it, it has come down to us unbroken. The original charter by which it was created, March 17th, 11 Edward III, differentiates the dukedom from the principality of Wales ; for whereas the title of Prince of Wales is conferred by special investiture by the King, the dukedom of Cornwall is vested indissolubly in the person of the eldest son of the reigning Sovereign. The Duchy Auditor who wrote an account of the Duchy for Henry, Prince of Wales, James I's elder son, in 1609 says : " The King's first begotten and eldest sons are as touching livery to be made unto them of the Duchy, accounted of full and perfect age, that is to say, of twenty-one years on the very day of their birth, so as even then in right, they ought to have livery thereof ". The Duchy is therefore a shifting possession from the Crown to the Duke and back to the Crown, for when the Duke dies or ascends the throne the Duchy reverts to the Sovereign. As Connock writes : " those honours and revenues are drowned again in the Crown ". During the dormancy of the dukedom the King functions " as he was Duke ", according to the formula.

There is this further legal peculiarity of the Duchy, that, since it was constituted by royal charter expressly forbidding the alienation of its lands, the Duke is unable to sever lands from it except with the consent of Parliament. And when lands were so severed, as in the case of

Henry VIII's annexation of the honour of Wallingford to the Crown — which previously was part of the Duchy — a number of monastic and other manors were granted instead, both within Cornwall and without, which were of equal or superior value. They were more conveniently administered as part of the Duchy since they lay in the west.

This process increased the number of manors of which the Duchy was comprised to some seventy-eight by the time of the Civil War, instead of the thirty-five with which it had been originally endowed at the time of its creation. They fell into several classes. There were, first, the seventeen " Antiqua Maneria " in Cornwall, which had formed part of the earldom ; secondly, there were the " Forinseca Maneria " outside the county, which were included by Edward III in his grant ; and, thirdly, the " Annexata Maneria ", both inside Cornwall and without, which had been incorporated subsequently by Act of Parliament. The original nucleus in Cornwall were the manors of Stokeclimsland, Rillaton, Helston-in-Trigg, Liskeard, Tybesta, Tywarnhaile, Talskedy, Penmayne, Calstock, Trematon, Restormel, Penkneth, Penlyne, Tewington, Helston-in-Kerrier, Tintagel, and Moresk. Upon these there existed a special conventionary form of tenure, from seven-year to seven-year, right up to the middle of the last century. The lands of the Duchy outside Cornwall were no less extensive than they were within, including an equal number of manors in various counties, and, as it still does, the honour of Bradninch, in Devonshire, all that high country between the rivers Exe and Culm, between Tiverton and Cullompton, and in London the manor of Kennington, upon which the Black Prince resided, now the most remunerative of all the Duchy's sources of income.

This being its peculiar constitution, the history of the dukedom has been one of dormancy in the Crown as much as of separate and independent existence under the Duke. The Black Prince, whose father, Edward III, lived such an unconscionably long time, enjoyed the Duchy for close on forty years ; but with his son, Richard II, who had no children, the Duchy lay dormant in the Crown. Under Henry IV, the later Henry V — Shakespeare's Prince Hal — was Duke ; then for the forty years from 1413 to 1453 the Duchy was again in the possession of the Crown, and there were lapses again in the fifteenth century.

With the death of Prince Arthur, Henry VII's elder son, in 1502, a new problem arose : did the King's surviving son and heir succeed to the Duchy under the charter ? Sir John Doddridge, whose little book on the Principality of Wales and the Duchy of Cornwall was published in 1630, says that the intention of the charter was " first that none should be Dukes of Cornwall, but such as were eldest sons and heirs apparent to the Crown ; and that when there was any fail of such person, then the said dignity should remain in suspense, until such son and heir apparent were extant ". But the lawyers interpreted the phrase the King's " eldest son " in the original charter to mean his eldest surviving son ; so that Henry, subsequently Henry VIII, was enabled to succeed to his brother's Duchy, as he did later to his wife. The precedent was followed in 1612, upon the death of Prince Henry, when his younger brother Charles succeeded.

But there were long periods in the sixteenth century when the Crown was in possession of the Duchy : under Henry VIII from 1509 till 1537, when his son Edward was born, and throughout the whole reigns of Edward, Mary, and Elizabeth — i.e. from 1547 to 1603. In the seventeenth century there were similar periods : under Charles I, from 1625 to 1645, when he handed over the government of the Duchy to his son ; under the Commonwealth, when the Duchy even ceased for a time to exist and its manors were sold. It was restored under Charles II, but there was no son to inherit the dukedom from 1649 right up to the death of Queen Anne in 1714, except for the brief and fugitive appearance of James II's infant son upon the public scene in 1688. The Hanoverians, being a more prolific stock, did their duty by the Duchy more regularly. The later George II was Duke from 1714 to 1727, then Frederick Prince of Wales from 1727 to 1751. There followed upon his death an interregnum until the later George IV was born in 1762. Again the Crown was in possession from 1820 to 1841, when the Prince who became Edward VII was born. From then right up to the accession of Edward VIII there has been a Duke of Cornwall, the longest continuous stretch in its history. With Edward VIII's accession the Duchy fell once more to the Crown, where it remains again until the birth of a son to the King. The remarkable feature of the dukedom historically, it will be observed, is its discontinuity, as compared with the virtually unbroken continuity of the Duchy.

Of the long line of its Dukes, few have been in a position to make acquaintance with, or take personal interest in, their Duchy. The first Duke, the Black Prince himself, owing to his length of tenure, was in a position to do so. Mr. Henderson says :

When the Black Prince came to man's estate and was renowned as a warrior all over Christendom, he paid more than one visit to his duchy. Restormel was his chief halting-place. . . . In May 1354, the Duchy Council wrote to John de Kendal, the receiver of Cornwall, ordering him to repair the castles in Cornwall, and especially the ' conduit ' in the castle of Restormel, as quickly as possible. In August following, the Prince himself came down to Cornwall, with a gallant company of Knights whose names are immortalised in the pages of Froissart.

Here the Prince remained from August 20th to about September 4th.

This was eight years after the Prince's first youthful campaign, which had culminated at Crécy, where he led the van and won his immortal name, to the English people, of the Black Prince. He was still only twenty-four on this first visit to the west. It was just before he was appointed lieutenant of Gascony, whence he made his famous marauding campaigns over the whole south of France, burning and ravaging as he went, and ending up with the famous victory at Poitiers, where he took the King of France prisoner.

Nine years after his first visit to the Duchy he paid another, at Eastertide 1363, to Restormel. He had been created Prince of Aquitaine and Gascony the year before, and was about to go abroad to take up his charge, which consumed all the remaining good years of his life in ceaseless war — altogether less fortunate than in his earlier years — in the south of France and upon the borders of Spain. He came home, wasted with disease, in 1371, but came no more to his Duchy. The Duchy went on as an administrative unit ; it had been strongly organised and its officers did not fail. During all these years they kept their books duly, and there remains to us as the fruit of their efforts that register dealing with the Prince's affairs in Cornwall known as the *White Book of Cornwall*, which reposes at the Public Record Office and has been published by His Majesty's Stationery Office as part of the *Black Prince's Register*.

From it we learn how the Prince's affairs in Cornwall were managed — how his revenues arose, the rents, fines, and profits of all kinds from his lands, the moneys arising from his stannary rights, the coinage of tin, the profits of his courts and all the innumerable small change of feudal tenure, the issues from wreck upon his manors on the coast. Then there were all the outgoings — payments to the Duchy's full complement of officers from the steward, sheriff, and receiver of the Duchy, the havenor who dealt with customs at the ports, the " Prince's batchelor and keeper of his game ", down to his keepers and bailiffs and chaplains. All the multifarious purposes, charitable and devotional or purely customary, of a great feudal landlord we find provided for : a chaplain to sing masses for the souls of the Prince's ancestors in the chapel of the castle at Trematon, another to sing for the souls of former Earls of Cornwall in the hermitage dedicated to the Holy Trinity in the park of Restormel ; it stood by the river-bank below the castle on the site of " Trinity " within earshot of the pleasant noise of the river rushing by outside. Then there were oaks to be given from the Duchy parks for pious purposes, to the Dominican Friars of Truro to build their church, to the Prior of Tywardreath, or to the parishioners of Stokeclimsland as a gift from the Prince to repair their church ; a grant of a tun of wine to a chaplain, or to a canon of Exeter going to keep his residence there the gift of " twelve does from this season of grease to be taken from the Prince's parks ".

The deer-parks were a very important part in the economy of the Duchy. When it was constituted there were seven : Kerrybullock (now Stokeclimsland), with 150 deer ; Liskeard Old Park, with 200 ; Lanteglos and Helsbury, with 180 ; Trematon, with 42 ; Restormel, with 300 ; and Launceston, with 15. After the Black Prince, the Dukes never visited their Duchy ; its castles tended to fall into disrepair and there was less point in maintaining the deer-parks efficiently. With the movement for enclosure that grew strong in the sixteenth century, Henry VIII decided to dispark the Duchy parks and turn them more profitably into pasture. It is the site of Kerrybullock Park, in the parish of Stokeclimsland, that the large Duchy farm now occupies.

The Duchy continued to be administered upon the lines laid down under the Black Prince ; it remained substantially the same through the generations.

Politicians and royal favourites came and went at remote Westminster ; dynasties changed ; there was civil war and battles raged upon English soil. Still the adminis-tration of the Duchy went on, the most permanent feature in the landscape of society in Cornwall, the diurnal routine of its tenants living close to the soil, undisturbed, unchanging, or changing slowly only with the slow tides of the ages. One derives the impression of an institution tenacious and conservative, one that neither relaxed its rights nor vexed its tenantry with new and unexpected impositions ; the fines it took upon leases remained stable over long periods. At bottom, it was the age-long reverence for custom and tradition, the bed - rock of human history, that prevailed and ruled in and through the Duchy.

The drastic social changes of the Reformation, how-ever, were not without their effect, and the Duchy emerged with a greater concentration of its lands in the west. Henry VIII detached the honours of Wallingford and St. Valery, but in exchange granted all the Cornish estates of the Earls of Devonshire, which fell to the Crown by the attainder of the Marquis of Exeter, some fifteen manors in all, and fifteen more Cornish manors belonging to the dissolved priories of Launceston and Tywardreath. This meant a considerable extension of Duchy lands into mid-Cornwall, though the main concentration still re-mained in the east of the county. In the far west, the farm of the Scilly Isles now became for the first time Duchy property. In the last years of Elizabeth, with the constant drain upon the finances of the long war with Spain, and the continuous campaigns in the Netherlands and Ireland, she found it necessary to sell eighteen of these newly-annexed manors. But it was held on James I's accession that the sale was illegal under the charter of the Duchy and the King recovered them.

Of the political influence of the Duchy in Cornwall in

these years, when its economic hold was so much strengthened, it is difficult to say much with certainty. It is the
popular view that the great increase which the Tudors
made in the parliamentary representation of Cornwall
was intended to assure and strengthen Royal influence
upon Parliament by the return of so many members —
forty-four in all — from a county where the Duchy had
such an extensive influence. But if that was the intention, it was not wholly fulfilled — at any rate, in the
sixteenth and seventeenth centuries. For in Elizabeth's
reign the Puritan leaders Peter and Paul Wentworth, the
initiators of parliamentary opposition, sat for Cornish
boroughs ; while in the reign of Charles I, at election after
election, the Duchy failed to get its candidates returned
against the local influence of Sir John Eliot, William
Coryton, and such Puritan and Parliamentarian families
as the Rouses of Halton.

With the outbreak of the Civil War the Duchy reached,
perhaps, the apex of its importance ; for upon its stable
and ordered administrative system, and upon its revenues,
Charles I had to fall back for the sinews of his cause in the
west. This most interesting phase of the Duchy's existence
has been studied most illuminatingly and in detail by Miss
Mary Coate in her *Cornwall in the Civil War*. In 1645, at
the decisive downward turn of his fortunes, Charles I took
the decision to grant livery of the Duchy to the young
Prince of Wales, then fifteen, and to send him into the
west with a Council attendant upon him, to govern the
west in his name. Hyde was the chief member of the
Prince's Council, and for a year he laboured hard to screw
up the resources of the Duchy and to stay the rot in the
Royalist forces. He was successful only in the first ; but
that at such a time of disintegration and defeat was a
remarkable achievement. The production of tin was
enormously increased and shipped across to France and
Holland to buy munitions. But nothing could stave off

the military defeat ; the Cavaliers were at daggers drawn among themselves, the Prince's Council was riddled with animosities and dissensions, and in March 1646 the Prince embarked at Falmouth for Scilly and later for France.

In these years Cornwall was being drained by both sides ; and no doubt it was the enormous sacrifices the county had made, both of man-power for the King — the Cornish army raised by Sir Bevil Grenville, which achieved such magnificent feats in the campaign of 1643, was bled white — and of its resources by both King and Parliament, that made Cornwall accept the Parliamentarian victory on the whole quietly and submissively. After so long a struggle, and such sacrifices made in vain, the ordinary Cornishman must have felt " A plague on both your houses ", and turned with satisfaction to beating the sword into a reaping-hook. It had been a great disadvantage, productive of much misery and impoverishment, for Cornwall to have been forced into such invidious prominence in the war by its association with the Duchy. However, the latter paid for the part it had played in the struggle. It was sold up by the victorious Parliament, its organisation dissolved. When Charles II came back to his throne all had to be reconstituted.

The old foundations, the old routine, however, were there ; it only remained to follow out their lines. The Duchy was revived, officers appointed ; at the head of them all was John Grenville, Earl of Bath, Sir Bevil's son, who as a lad of sixteen, when his father was killed at Lansdown, was lifted on to his horse to take his place and encourage the dispirited Cornish foot. The close personal friend of the King — he shared his room in the palace at Whitehall, and later was, with the Earl of Feversham, the only Protestant present when the dying Charles was received into the Roman Church — now in 1661 he was made High Steward of the Duchy, Lord Warden of the Stannaries, Rider and Master of Dartmoor Forest, offices which went with the Duchy, and later Lord Lieutenant of Cornwall. The age-long customs of the Duchy, temporarily stilled, woke again to their slow, satisfying routine ; the manor courts were held in the King's name, the Lord Warden came down in person to preside at the Parliament of the Stannaries ; the tin trade flourished ; there was money once more for Charles to support his mistresses at Whitehall.

With the Duchy settling again into its old accustomed routine, there remains only to notice the stannaries, from which the Duchy had early drawn some part of its revenues. With the greatly increasing return from the mines of Cornwall, this source of revenue was expanding and becoming ever more important. After the Restoration the history of the Duchy is without constitutional excitements, and the economic factor of the stannaries becomes more prominent. Theirs is a history distinct from, though subordinate to, the Duchy ; it has been treated in full by Dr. G. R. Lewis in his book *The Stannaries*. Nevertheless, the popular view of what the stannaries were is even less clear than as to the Duchy : a recent article on the latter, almost the only one to appear, referred to the stannaries as " tin mines ", which they were not. They were areas of jurisdiction covering not only the tin mines, but the whole of the tin industry and all affairs arising out of it. They formed a peculiar jurisdiction springing from the Royal prerogative in the working of metals. As such they were not subject to common law ; after many disputes on the point, the leading case of Trewynnard in the reign of Elizabeth decided that there was no appeal from the stannary courts to the ordinary courts of law. They had their own system of courts with an ultimate appeal to the Council of the Prince as Duke of Cornwall. It is worth noting that the last survival of the ancient stannary courts remained until as late as 1896, when the court of the Vice-Warden of the Stannaries was abolished.

When the Duchy was created in 1337 the stannaries of Cornwall and Devon were incorporated into it ; from that time the Duke took the place of the King in receiving their revenues and regulating their affairs. His Council formed the fountain-head of all stannary administration. He appointed the Lord Warden to act as his representative in governing the stannaries, naming their officers, summoning the tinners' parliaments, assenting to their legislation, promulgating new laws and enactments for their regulation. As a peculiar jurisdiction with its own rights, the stannaries mustered their own men for service in times of danger. In the alarming years before and after the Spanish Armada we find frequent complaints from the deputy-lieutenants of Cornwall against the stannaries on the ground of the overlapping of jurisdictions and their consequent inability to make complete returns of men for the musters. But Sir Walter Raleigh's position as Lord Warden was sufficient to maintain the independence of the stannaries from the ordinary local administration, and co-ordination of the two was usually provided for by the appointment of the Lord Warden as lord lieutenant of the county.

With the great development of the mining industry in Cornwall in the eighteenth century the revenues from the stannary must have become an increasing part of the revenues of the Duchy. Complicated as it would be to work out in detail, it is not difficult to sum up what the economic effect of the Duchy has been upon Cornwall through the centuries. It must have meant, on balance, a constant and very serious drain of wealth from a county which was, except for its minerals, poor in resources. Charles Henderson, our chief authority on Cornish history, held this to be the reason why so few large estates were formed in Cornwall, and why, charming as a number of the Cornish country houses are, there are not many historic houses to compare with those of other counties.

That pleasant antiquary, Richard Carew of Antony, who wrote his *Survey of Cornwall* towards the end of Elizabeth's reign, and in such delightful Elizabethan English, comments a little sadly upon there being no Cornish peerage in his time, no one in Cornwall, of however ancient a family, whom the Queen might call cousin.

Under the Hanoverian dynasty the Duchy went on according to its old-established order ; though I do not know that any of the first four Georges paid any personal visits to their Duchy. All our recent sovereigns from Victoria onwards have done so. Edward VII as Prince of Wales visited his Cornish estates on several occasions. The revenues which accumulated during his minority enabled him to buy Sandringham, as they enabled Edward VIII when Duke to buy Fort Belvedere.

Perhaps it was in consequence of this, or as an indication of the distinction he wished to maintain between his capacity as Duke of Cornwall and his public rôle as Prince and King, or simply out of sentiment for the Duchy, that the Duchy of Cornwall flag was always flown at Fort Belvedere and never any other. At any rate, Cornishmen may hope so, with images of the Duchy in their mind — the centuries-old buildings going back to Edmund Earl of Cornwall, by the quayside at Lostwithiel, lapped by the tidal waters of the river Fowey ; the house at Trematon within the old walls of the castle, where Sir Richard Grenville, grandfather of the hero, took refuge in the time of the great " Commotion " of 1549, the castle to which Drake took the treasure which he brought home from his voyage round the world, the grey walls now looking quietly down through the twinkling leaves to the broad waters of the Hamoaze and across to Devonport ; or Launceston Castle, with the ruined shell of its keep ; or Tintagel, grim, barbaric upon its desolate headland, the inspiration of so much poetry and legend. Whether one thinks of these, or the delightful acres of pasture and woodland, the small enclosed fields within their granite hedges, the long, slow, laborious lives of the generations, the farmers and their strong sons serving the Duchy, tilling the soil, it is all the same. Not a Cornishman but must have felt some catch at the heart when the flag with the fifteen gold bezants was broken for the last time at Fort Belvedere, not only for the gesture in itself, but for all the history that lies behind it.

RIALTON: A CORNISH
MONASTIC MANOR

BEHIND the hideous, unhappy mess that the specu-
lative builder has made of modern Newquay there
is a delicious valley, in the old-fashioned Cornish
manner, that runs down to the sea at St. Columb Porth.
A narrow winding road, with innumerable twists and
bends, a little stream that goes singing down through
the meadows bright with golden flag and meadow-sweet,
the low hills upheaved on either hand, a good deal of
rough brake beside the ploughland, and along the road
as you go the characteristic groups of tiny Cornish elms,
the hedges in early summer coloured with purple vetch
and crowsfoot, the first foxgloves and pink campion. And
over all there is the rumour, the magic presence, of the
sea, invisible yet always there.[1]

At one of the bends in the road is Rialton. You
wouldn't think anything of it at first view : just a Cornish
stone cottage, rather larger than usual. The house turns
its back on the road, at the end of a real cottage garden,
full of primulas in spring, of phloxes and sweet-william
in summer. It is not until you go up the cobbled path
and round to the old front of the house that you see what
an interesting place it is, very Cornish and at the same
time a rare survival for Cornwall. For what you are face
to face with is a fragment, the main front of a late fifteenth-
century or early Tudor house, a monastic manor.

The place indeed has a long and interesting history.
From early Celtic times it was the chief possession of
Bodmin Priory, the jewel among the lands of those canons,
fat or lean. It was the capital of their hundred of Pydar-

---

[1] Since writing this, in 1941, I am told that road-widening operations,
by the County Council, have done their best to spoil the valley.

shire, which means, of course, Petrockshire, St. Petrock having been the apostle of all this neighbourhood in the age of the saints, and the patron saint of Bodmin Priory. It appears in Domesday Book, when there were seven hides of land in the manor requiring 30 plough teams ; the canons kept two hides in demesne and one plough team. The villeins had the remaining hides and 11 plough teams. There were 30 villeins, 15 bordars, two serfs, and 20 sheep. There were 60 acres of wood and 300 acres of pasture. The yearly value was £4 : a lot at that time, especially for Cornwall. So throughout the quiet Middle Ages it sustained the lazy, praying monks miles away at Bodmin.

There must always have been something of a manor house here ; but at the turn of the sixteenth century the priors of Bodmin, following the fashion of their greater colleagues at Glastonbury and elsewhere, with an eye for a delectable spot for a country residence, turned it into a comfortable mansion. The main part of this house remains, though changed about internally : the medieval hall and kitchen with its solar, the fine medieval wagon roof such as you see in so many Cornish churches. Then came Prior Vyvyan, the last but one of the long line that bore rule at Bodmin, who added the wide porch with the study above, which is the chief feature of the house externally. It has a fine mullioned window of six lights, in two of them fragments of glass with the prior's initials *T. V.* and the arms of the priory, the three fishes ; next to it is the prior's oratory, or bed-chamber, with its window also looking out over the courtyard to the meadows and orchards of the south, the elms that fringe the hillside. A very suitable retreat for an ecclesiastic burdened with so much business, the sound of the sea thundering upon that coast subdued to a murmur in the quiet valley, the stream running by to accompany his prayers and meditations.

Thomas Vyvyan, Prior of Bodmin and titular Bishop of Megara, was a forceful personage and much the most important churchman in Cornwall upon the threshold of the Reformation. He was a sort of local counterpart to Wolsey, with whom his career was roughly contemporary. With him bearing rule at Bodmin, it was as if Cornwall had its own bishop, as in the days before ever Exeter was a see at all. A Cornishman himself, and the holder of much preferment in the county, he was the last figure, on the grand scale, who embodied the old order. When he died and was buried in the magnificent Renaissance tomb which stood before the high altar of the priory church and was later shifted to the parish church — fortunately, for nothing of the priory remains — men must have felt that the old order was changing. It was. Prior Vyvyan died on Pentecost Sunday, June 1st, 1533. Within six years the priory was down, Rialton, the apple of his eye, granted away to a layman, brother of his successor, the last prior.

It was the manner of its doing that was so interesting : it provides a very nice example of what was going on in the monasteries at the end, the scurry to lease away properties to relatives, to make friends with the outer world before being thrown upon it.

When Prior Vyvyan lay on his deathbed, he declared, according to his steward Nicholas Prideaux, that " none of his brethren, being canons of the said priory, was meet and able to be prior there and to succeed him ". Nevertheless, in spite of this reported ill-opinion of them, the brethren met according to custom in the chapel of the Virgin and elected one of themselves his successor. Prideaux stated many years later that the dying prior had desired him to do all he could to get Thomas Mundy (*alias* Wandsworth), then a canon at Merton Abbey in Surrey, elected. This may have been a fabrication. Mundy belonged to a well-known family in the City of London —

they were an old Cheshire family originally — which had provided a Lord Mayor and must have been known to Cromwell. Cromwell insisted on his man being appointed, and shortly after we find Brother Symons, the shadow-prior of a few months, retired on a fat pension. Mundy was elected ; he was a good man of business, and it is not long before we find rewards going up to London to the all-powerful Secretary and his servants. First it is an annuity of five marks for Cromwell's servant, eight congers for his master, and " if anything in Cornwall can do your pleasure you may command me ". The prior then helps Cromwell's servant in conveying his hawks and hounds, two falcons, three merlins, a brace of greyhounds, " a fair dog and a mean bitch ". More important, a patent goes up to Cromwell for an annuity of £6 for life. (Multiply by 20 or 25 for a contemporary valuation. And Cromwell would be the recipient of some scores of such favours.)

Nicholas Prideaux received his reward for his part in bringing about Mundy's election : the lease of the great tithes of the four parishes, Egloshayle, St. Minver, St. Cubert, and Padstow, the district round the Camel estuary, for a very long period of years at a reduced rent. This was the foundation of the Prideaux holding in that neighbourhood ; the monastic " place ", the tithe-barn of the monks, became that fine Elizabethan house, Place at Padstow, built in the year of the Armada, and looking from its splendid situation south out over the inland lake of the estuary, now blue, now green, now lavender in the declining sun. The association between the prior and Prideaux went much further than that. Before they finished, these two old bachelors — it was really Prideaux's scheme — had excogitated a complicated dynastic structure by which the two families were to be knit together. Various respective nephews and nieces were to be married and provided for by monastic leases. It was very pretty. It was the Prideaux family that ultimately came out on top.

But the prior did very well for his family too. To his elder brother John, whom he brought into Cornwall, he granted a lease of Rialton for no fewer than 99 years at £60 per annum, a rent much less than it was worth. Henry VIII made it illegal for these long leases to be granted within a year from the Dissolution ; the normal term for a Crown property was 21 years, and these long leases meant that the Crown was cheated out of large payments on renewal of them. Those sums, in addition to the reduced rent, meant a substantial capital gift to John Mundy. His son and heir was to marry Prideaux's niece Elizabeth, when she came of age, in consideration of which the prior granted them the manor of Padstow, with its rights, such as the wreck of the sea, for 90 years. Elizabeth's name was put into the Rialton lease ; but somehow she and William got out of marrying each other. However, her brother and his sister, William Prideaux and Joan Mundy, were married off upon the prior's supplying the cash.

And so the Mundys came to Rialton. Five generations of them lived in the house and married among Cornish families. John and William were succeeded by another John, he by his son Thomas, and Thomas by a third John, who was the last of them there. They were prolific enough ; but the fact that the property was leasehold, and its ownership vested in the Duchy of Cornwall by Henry VIII's Act, meant that the Mundys could not be sure of rooting themselves, and in fact they were uprooted by the Commonwealth. The very extensive manor was then worth £204 per annum. A cloud had rested on their tenure from the very beginning, owing to the circumstances of the lease ; and there was a good deal of litigation in Edward VI's reign and in Elizabeth's before their hold was confirmed. No doubt it cost them some money.

The family did not make much of a show in Cornwall ; they took their place among the lesser gentry. They may have had Catholic sympathies : a son of the house, Francis, was educated at Leyden, became a priest, and was drowned off Leghorn in 1655. An offshoot of the family at Penryn produced Peter Mundy, the traveller. But he is a story to himself.

After the Mundys it does not seem that the Godolphins, to whom the lease was granted, lived there, though Sidney, the first Earl, took the second title of Viscount Rialton. The house descended to being a farm. Then about seventy years ago the Duchy built a large new farmhouse farther up the valley on higher ground, Rialton Barton ; Rialton descended further to becoming Rialton Mill. Practically all the east wing, the service wing, was demolished. Two very fine perpendicular stone archways found their way to the barton. On one there are the words *S. Petrocus*, with the initials *T. V.* and perhaps his arms ; the arch is inscribed *Rialtoun* and *T. V. Prior Hoc Fecit*, together with the arms of England and of the priory, with the motto *Sit Laus Deo*.

It would seem that the old house consisted of the main wing, containing hall and kitchen, solar and prior's chamber and oratory, with the porch, and a service wing at right angles on the east side of the courtyard. Something of the inner wall of the latter with a little blocked archway remains, behind the well in the courtyard ; it is a pretty little canopied holy well, with a niche for the saint in the back wall. But it needs clearing of ivy and strengthening. Close to the well is a granite archway giving entrance to the court : perhaps the remains of a vanished gate-house. There were no doubt more out-buildings ; a curious woodcut in Gilbert's *History* shows Rialton with three gateways.

The interior of the house certainly has its charm. The stone-vaulted entry with its granite bosses is now blocked up ; on either side is a little closet in the wall, porter's lodge or strong room. That on the left with its tiny quatrefoil ventilator they call the dungeon. The interior arrangements of the house have been much changed : a floor inserted dividing the hall into two storeys, though upstairs the fine wagon roof still remains. So does that of the solar. A new front door and staircase leads up in the centre of the old hall. Still, fragment as it is, the main part of the house remains, in its delightful situation. But what an interesting piece of work it would be — old houses are rare in Cornwall, and this in its way is unique — to take it in hand, rebuild the destroyed wing and restore the house to its former pleasant shape. It would be a labour of love for someone, and very rewarding : it has such possibilities.

I confess that when I think of Rialton I do not think of the Mundys. It is always the same image that comes into my mind's eye : that of Prior Vyvyan riding his Cornish nag along that winding road coming from Bodmin, his face the bland, powerful visage of the ecclesiastic lying upon his tomb in Bodmin Church, mitred, jewelled, the headless angels holding up the shields of his arms about him through the long nights and days.

THE STORY OF POLRUDDON[1]

I WENT the other evening for a walk from my house in pursuit of a ghost. Or rather, not of a ghost in the ordinary sense, but of an historic shade. For the man whom I was in pursuit of once had an actual historic existence, and I do not know that he has haunted anyone or anywhere — even the place that was his when he was alive — in the four and a half centuries that have gone by since he disappeared. But what I found was the ghost of a place.

There is nothing more warming to the imagination, or that adds more savour to living in the country, than to come upon the track of interesting memories, stories, traditions attached to some place right under your nose when you never suspected their existence. It is always happening to me within the bounds of my own parish, or just around it — while Cornwall as a whole is a world, is more than America. That is what makes inhabiting it so satisfying, to anyone with imagination and a sense of history.

As recently as when I wrote *Tudor Cornwall* I never knew that there was this little place within two or three miles of my home with this interesting happening attached to it — of the Tudor time, too — or I would have made some mention of it. It is an incident so characteristic of the late Middle Age and with its own pathos. Nor does anyone else know of it. It must be centuries since anyone living even near by knew of the story attached to the house. I did not know if there was a house there, or what to expect when I got there.

So I set out from my home — the pleasant low-eaved house next to the disused mine that is now a cornfield,

[1] Pronounce Polreddon. (The "u" is a Cornish *u*; cf. Carluddon.)

with the lovely line of beeches leading down to the sea and the wood where haunt the green woodpecker, the magpie, and the jay — up the hill above Porthpean, past the white gate and the woods of Penrice to the four turnings at Lobb's shop. (Who the original Lobb was, I wish I knew ; but evidently his was a blacksmith's shop.) To the left goes the road to adorable Trenarren and the headland ; to the right the lane to Towan, once the head farm of the Duchy's great manor of Tewington, which covered much of this neighbourhood ; ahead the narrow winding road or rather lane — but here all roads wind and are no more than lanes — that leads to Pentewan, with its little harbour and grand Regency Terrace looking down upon the nest of roofs, now all repaired from that recent event so characteristic of the twentieth century.

This is the most delicious of lanes, the hedges always flowered and awake with life. For whole stretches there are long rabbit-runs along the top of the earth hedge, up-heavals large enough for foxes' or badgers' earths. Here in the gateway is a small half-wild cat waiting for some prey or other, bird or dormouse. Though it is early in August, the honeysuckle, which grows in rich waxy bushes along this road, is already mostly over, for the flowers are earlier in Cornwall. In these deep-sheltered lanes, warm and wet and southern, there is a profusion of ferns and flowers. The foxgloves are over, the golden ragwort has taken their place, with its rich starry clusters of warm yellow like butter. Then there is blue scabious and purple-horned wood-bettany, willowy mullins and fre-quent yarrow. Nothing very rare that I notice, a patch of tiny pink thyme, plenty of burdock in flower ; and everywhere the fresh green of new fern-growth, hart's-tongue and maidenhair, with its infinitely satisfying earthy smell.

So, day-dreaming, the eye almost unconsciously registering the flowers, I come to my favourite spot in this walk : where there is a sharp bend in the road and a depression, a valley so diminutive you can hardly call it a valley at all. And yet it has a totally different atmosphere. I don't know what there is about it ; I always long to know its name ; but I don't believe it has one, for there is no house near by and it is just nowhere at all. There is a gate and a flat, enclosed, meadowy little paddock, with a stream and trees all round : beautiful little Cornish elms, self-sown, in a screen, a few ashes and sycamores. There is the scent of cut sycamores hanging in the air. When you put your head over that gate, it is as if you are breaking in upon a secret enchantment, as if you had surprised — well, what ? There is only a little meadow there, and the stream that has made this magic valley on its way to the sea. Nothing else ; only the swift silvery music of the summer flies in the evening light under the sycamores.

It is an enchanted spot : just such a place as would seduce the heart of M. le Sous-Préfet aux Champs. Just such a place as Pan might haunt with his pipe, or some Celtic spirit of field and wood and water, some earlier chthonic god of fertility, who still watches over his moon-lit rites by the stream.

I mount the hill between Polglaze away on the right among its trees (the name means " the green pool ") and Porthtowan on the left towards the coast. There is the long grey line of the old farm-house rising among the tufted greenery. It takes its name from the beach at the foot of the cliff : " the beach of the sandhills ". And now I am at the top of the hill at the gate that looks back over the coast to the east, on this clear summer evening, to Plymouth and beyond. There in the foreground is the lizard neck of Black Head ; across the other side of the bay, the Gribbin, its full length extended to the west and the sun, the lovely spaced cloud-shadows along it, blue in colour, the coves looking incredibly near ; beyond, the inlet of Fowey (the thought of dear Q., as always when I look across the hills that way : the fact that he is no longer *there* does not make so much difference, he is so bound up with it all for ever). Then Lantivet Bay with its grim memory, the cliffs about Looe, the long curve of White-sand Bay, terminating in the conical hill of Rame Head, which appears so often in Hakluyt, in those mariners' accounts of their Elizabethan voyages outward or home-ward bound : it must have been a loved landmark to them, to many of them the last bit of their native land they saw, the first to welcome them home to Plymouth Sound.

For John Polruddon there was no homecoming. I look down upon the little fields that once were his : the yellow-green one from which the corn has been shaven, the rough tussocked paddock with a pony cropping, on the shoulder of the little hill that rises above the creek of Pentewan.

This must be Polruddon. But how to get there ? There is no entrance : just a gate leading into the fields, a shed on the right among the furze bushes. I open the gate with some trepidation : the old fear of tres-passing, ingrained from childhood, mixed with another excitement — what should I find there ? Should I be disappointed ?

My feet follow the rocky path down the slope to where I see a cluster of old grey buildings. I come out upon a green platform, where cows are cropping, which looks direct upon the sea. But where is the farm-house ? There are outbuildings and, beyond, what might be a hind's cottage ; but no farm-house. I am baffled by the place. There are a few starved-looking cats about the farmyard, some starveling chickens scratching among the stones. Then a dog, and shortly after its master appears : an oldish-looking labourer with a vacant eye, who is so much of a piece with the place he might be an emanation of it.

The *genius loci*, a natural. He hardly understands what I say to him. " Where is the house ? " There is no house. Is that the farm-house ? I ask, pointing to the improbable-looking tumble-down dwelling at the end of the farmyard. No ; a cowshed. Does no one live here, then ? No, nobody lives there.

That was the answer. The place was deserted.

I told the old man, who had attached himself to me, why I had come. Were there no remains of the old house at all ? Some gleam of perception came into the wintry grey eye — there was something satyr-like in the expression — of my hardly articulate companion in this desolate spot. Not altogether at ease, I followed him into the cattle-shed, of which he unbarred the door for me.

There, unmistakably, were relics of the Tudor house : a fine great open fireplace of shaped and moulded moorstone ; above it, a similar but smaller fireplace ; the wooden beam one of the original ones, massive and worm-eaten, but still keeping the roof up. That was all.

What could the building have been ? A part of the original hall ? How explain the two fireplaces, one above the other ? I could not make it out.

We came out into the farmyard that was also a platform, and I saw that it was really the *emplacement* of a fine house looking to the sea. An improvident man, John Polruddon, to have built so boldly, and apparently so finely, right there on the edge of the cliff. It was asking for trouble, in those disturbed days of the late fifteenth century. And trouble was not long in coming, for him and his house.

The story of Polruddon is told by Norden in his *Description of Cornwall*, dedicated to James I : he must have gathered it when he was down here collecting material for his book :

Polruddon, the Ruynes of an auntient howse, somtymes the howse of John Polruddon, whoe was taken out of his bed by the Frenche in the time of Henry the 7 and caried away with violence ; and then began the howse to decaye, and Penwarne the howse of M. Otwell Hill, was buylded with Polruddon stones. The howse (as by the ruynes it appeareth) was a fayre howse, and by the arched fresstone windowes which it had curiouslye wrowghte testifieth it to be for the time elegant. Nere this Polruddon is the beste freestone that Cornwall yeildeth, and the moste of the churches and towres therabout were buylded of them. There is nere the ruyns of this howse, under Polruddon hill, a wounderfull deepe hole or Cave, which the Welshe call an *Ogo*, the Cornishe a *Googoo*, which passeth under the grounde so farr as the ende can no man finde, as is sayde.

Carew tells us nothing of this story ; but he tells us of a similar happening in the parish of Talland. One of the ancestors of Master Murth, he says,

within the memorie of a next neighbour to the house, called Prake, (burdened with 110 yeeres age) entertained a British [*i.e.* Breton] miller, as that people, for such idle occupations, prove more hardie, then our owne. But this fellowes service befell commodious in the worst sense. For when, not long after his acceptance, warres grewe betweene us and France, he stealeth over into his countrey, returneth privily backe againe, with a French crew, surprizeth suddenly his master, and his ghests, at a Christmas supper, carrieth them speedily unto Lantreghey [*i.e.* Tréguier], and forceth the Gent. to redeeme his enlargement, with the sale of a great part of his revenewes.

How little things change in human history ! It might be Nazi technique in the twentieth century.

John Polruddon was not (I fancy) of an old family ; he seems to have made his position for himself. He would certainly think of himself rather as an ancestor — building the finest house in these parts out there upon those cliffs for his family to take root in — before the swift blow came out of the sea that dark night and scattered all. I have a suggestion to put forward about him : that his fortune came from the famous quarry of Pentewan stone in the cliffs next Polruddon. The finest fifteenth-century churches of the district are built of this stone : the splendid and richly decorated tower of St. Austell with its symbols of the Trinity, its images of the Saints, traditionally finished in the year of the 1497 Rising ; Bodmin church, the noblest of Cornish churches in space and proportion, of which we still have the building accounts. The stone went direct by ship across the bay to St. Blazey and then overland up the valley to Bodmin. It may have been remunerative to John Polruddon, and it was a fine house that he built himself of the stone ready there on the spot.

Now the sun was gone behind the hill. There was a shadow over the place. The evening blue of the sea was cold, unfriendly. I shivered a little and was ready to go, wondering as I went back up the hill why it was that John Polruddon never returned. Had he been unable to raise the ransom for his release ? Was he killed in some scuffle on board ship, or in the street of some Breton town, Tréguier, or Roscoff, or Ploërmel, in trying to escape ? Or, more curious, did he find release from the burden of family and possessions a welcome thing, and *choose* never to come home again ? That would be a very Cornish theme — so many of the miners who left home in the great emigration of the eighteen-seventies and eighties did just that. Perhaps he found a new life abroad, went adventuring like young Peter Carew in the French wars in Italy, or Richard Grenville in the war in Hungary, or Champernowne and Raleigh in the French Wars of Religion in Normandy and Poitou.

All one could be certain of, looking back upon Polruddon in the gathering shades — pathetic, deserted little place with its few stunted trees and sparse bushes of elder and ash — was that ship coming out of the darkness, the scramble up the cliff, the sudden descent upon the house, the cries of women and children, the father carried off to

France in the greyness of dawn. And so John Polruddon, who might have founded the leading family in these parts and left a name, slips out of history.

But though that is the end of his house, it is not the end of the stones that he brought together. Norden has told us that in Elizabeth's time Otwell Hill quarried from them to build Penwarne, that fine old farm-house with its hall and porch and buttery in antiquated medieval style, near Mevagissey. You may see Master Hill and his wife lying uncomfortably upon their elbows, one above the other, on their monument next the altar in Mevagissey church. They have been lying there like that since the reign of James I. They were succeeded by their nephew, John Carew, Richard Carew's gallant son, whose hand was shot off by a cannon-ball at the siege of Ostend in 1601. Coming back to his lodgings, the story goes, he threw his hand upon the table saying, " This is the hand that cut the pudding today." He had made for himself a curiously contrived mechanical hand of iron that worked with springs ; and this still exists — a somewhat macabre object that yet links up with the heroic struggle of the Netherlands for freedom — among the heirlooms of the Tremaynes of Heligan.

Still the site was not deserted. What remained of the house was reconstructed by one of the Scobells of Menagwins, a generation later. It came into the possession of Henry Scobell, Clerk of the Parliament during the Commonwealth. He must have known its story. It is curious to think of that sedate political personage — a busy Puritan bureaucrat, prudent and impersonal, the colleague of Thurloe and Bradshaw and an intimate of the Protector's circle — living out on this cliff. But it is improbable that he saw much of the place during those crowded years in Westminster, amid all the crises of State, and in the intervals publishing voluminously upon the laws of that Parliament the great Protector was making superfluous. Scobell saw his cause fall into ruins, even as his house was to do ; and in the midst of the ruin he died.

Polruddon continued in the hands of his family and its representatives all through the eighteenth century ; and then, it seems, a fire consumed it.

Being at Pentewan one day I climbed the hill to have a look at the Terrace. It has a pleasant Regency appearance, the stonework of the houses framed in a stucco colonnade running along the front. But when close up to it, I noticed that the windows and doorways were unmistakably of the sixteenth or seventeenth century. They had come — as an old Terrace lady confirmed — from the house over the hill.

And that is all there is of Polruddon now : a few stones, the empty *emplacement* on that seaward-looking platform — like John Carew's iron hand, or Henry Scobell's learned law-books, so many *disjecta membra* of time. And yet it gives me a curious pleasure to have brought back even so much of John Polruddon, whose story no one among the neighbouring folk had remembered for generations, to have given him once more a local habitation and a name.

CORNWALL IN THE CIVIL WAR

THERE is no more fascinating occupation than the game of reconstructing the look of the English countryside as it was in previous centuries, under the hide of the modern world and beneath the accretions that time has brought. And with no part of the country is it a more attractive pursuit than with Cornwall. For one thing, the county has much changed ; it has become popular ; the making of roads and railways has had a greater influence here than elsewhere in drawing the country together into a whole — as Cavour said of Italy, the railways would " stitch the boot together in time ". And so they have ; the immobility of the old inhabitants, which lasted right up to the last generation, has come to an end with this ; innumerable visitors flood into the county with every summer — fortunately, for in the decline of mining and fishing it has become the only dependable and prosperous industry ; there has been much building, almost always of an injudicious and taste-less character, and perhaps as much destruction of what was ancient and beautiful.

Yet, in spite of all time's ruin, the careful observer with a sense of the past will be able to find, what the many following the beaten tracks will miss, the speaking remains of an earlier generation, fragments of a vanished yet moving age. He may easily, with a little of the gift of historical imagination, construct a picture in his mind of the Cornwall that knew Sir Bevil Grenville and Sidney Godolphin — there were never two more achieved and lovely characters in all that time of men of good report; of Cornwall in the year that the Lord General came down with his army to meet its fate upon the narrow neck of land between Lostwithiel and the sea, and when the

King slept all night in his coach in the park at Boconnoc, surrounded by his guards.

True, nothing remains of the great house of Stowe, where Sir Richard Grenville of the Azores lived — " my poore howse of Stowe ", he usually writes in a propitiatory way to the Council when he has to excuse himself for some ill-behaviour — and which Sir Bevil was engaged in beautifying with damask for the hall and "Turkey work" and pictures and new mullioned windows in the years before the Civil War; by the end of the century it had become the greatest house in the West Country. But there is Lanhydrock House, which remains much as the Lord Robartes built it in the years of his enforced retirement from affairs, with its formal garden and gate-house and the great double avenue of beeches and chest-nuts beyond sloping down the valley to the Prince's castle of Restormel ; or Godolphin in the far west, not far from the Land's End — that house with the granite colonnade and the long gallery above it, now lonely and deserted by the Godolphins after all the generations of them that lived there once. Yet these are, in a way, on a main, if not the beaten, track ; whereas the most pertinacious of travellers would hardly run down Erisey Barton, so remote it is, hidden away in a fork from the high road across Goonhilly Downs to the Lizard, now an old forlorn farm-house that yet retains the grand new doorway that Richard Erisey made when he brought his young wife home to the house in 1620, and the noble upstanding pillars giving on to the forecourt that were put up in 1672, in the twelfth year of the King's return to his own.

This is the Cornwall that one has in mind in reading Miss Coate's book,[1] which treats as it never has been done before the history of the county in the disturbed, the exciting years from the Civil War to the Restoration.

[1] *Cornwall in the Great Civil War and Interregnum, 1642–1660*, by Mary Coate, 1933.

Miss Coate claims, and with reason, that it is the most important period in all Cornish history :

> The period of the Civil Wars and Interregnum is the most important in the history of Cornwall, for never before or since has she contributed so largely to the general course of events. The creation and success of the Cornish army in 1643 and the defeat of Essex in 1644, the prolonged resistance to the New Model Army in 1645, and the persistent Royalism of the Cornish gentry under the Protectorate, all directly influenced the history of England as a whole. From 1640 to 1660 Cornwall was never negligible ; every Government had to reckon with its high-spirited people and felt obliged to watch it carefully. Consequently the history of Cornwall in this period has more than a local interest and importance. It belongs to the realm of the historian rather than of the antiquarian.

With reason : yet it is a claim that requires qualification. For if it is true that Cornwall in the Middle Ages was too unimportant, too much shut up in its own remote life, to influence events in the country at large, the same cannot be said of its history in the Tudor period : a century that saw an army of Cornishmen march from one end of the country to the other in 1497, until it met with defeat only upon Blackheath, and that witnessed the dangerous Rebellion of 1549, which paralysed government for a time and ultimately led to the downfall of the Protector Somerset.

The sixteenth century was the heyday of Cornwall in the national economy and in the national strategy — by 1625, Miss Coate states, it was declining in prosperity ; under the Tudors it was not only a chief repository of the nation's known mineral wealth but became the front line of defence as naval warfare moved away from France and the narrow seas to the outer seas and Spain. The defence of the country concentrated around the entrance to the Channel ; Henry VIII built Pendennis Castle and St. Mawes (that perfect relic of the age, a trefoil of walls now standing silver-grey among flower-beds and lawns running down to the sea) to guard the entrance to Falmouth harbour : Henry, Edward, and Elizabeth all spent large sums upon fortifying the Scilly Islands and maintaining garrisons there : while under Drake's strong hand, Plymouth was turned into the most powerful fortress in the West. From these ports, too, sailed most of the voyages of discovery, of Hawkins, Drake, Frobisher and Raleigh, no less than the great naval expeditions like the Drake-Norris attack on Lisbon in 1589 in reply to the Armada, and the Cadiz Expedition of 1596. Naturally, too, the sporadic raiding in retaliation fell upon the Cornish coasts ; and it was chiefly Westerners who languished in Spanish prisons. In short, Cornwall was in the forefront of the war ; and it is this that explains the rapidity and ease of the transition to Protestantism under Elizabeth, after the belated resistance to it under Edward VI and the pathetic adherence to Catholicism shown in the Prayer-book Rising.

This may account for the large number of Parliamentary boroughs (fifteen between 1545 and 1603) enfranchised by the Tudors, a representation which became out of all proportion to the county's importance in the nation later on, but was not so unrepresentative at the time. This question has always been something of a problem to the historian ; Miss Coate does much to clear it up in one of the best sections of her book. Mr. W. P. Courtney held the view, in his *Parliamentary Representation of Cornwall*, that these creations were a deliberate attempt on the part of the Crown to pack Parliament with thirty new members elected from a county peculiarly under Royal control. But this neglected the fact that the Tudors had little need to pack Parliament, they were so much of the same mind as the classes which sent members there. Miss Coate explains it by saying, " It seems more probable that the Tudors enfranchised the fifteen Cornish boroughs to please the landed gentry and the local townsmen, now in close partnership ".

As is well known, the Cornish members took as independent a line as any other body of members in the House, and were even more responsible than most for the development of Parliamentary opposition to the Crown. Peter Wentworth, the originator of its technique, was member for Tregony, and was not the sainted Sir John Eliot (harsh doctrinaire that he was) the martyr of the Parliamentary cause ? The attitude of the average Cornish member may be summed up in William Coryton's phrase, " I sought to God by my prayers and then searched the Statutes ". (How like the temper of Cromwell's " Trust in God and keep your powder dry " : the element common to both propositions may be taken for granted.) So that, when the Civil War broke out, it was not to be expected but that a strong Parliamentarian party would declare itself in the county against the Royalists. If the King had on his side such men as Sir Bevil Grenville, Sir Richard Vyvyan, Francis Basset, John Arundell of Trerice, and Lord Mohun, the Parliament had the support of Lord Robartes, Sir Richard Buller, John St. Aubyn, Francis Rous, the Carews and Boscawens ; and, as the Royalist historian Joseph Jane avers, they were " a passionate company ".

Moreover, families here, as elsewhere, were divided. Sir Bevil Grenville was the heart and soul of the King's cause, but his brother Richard was a deserter from the Parliament ; and, as Miss Coate says, " If nine Arundells rode in arms for the King, two, Thomas and Francis, were for the Parliament ; Sir Francis Godolphin of Godolphin and his brother Sidney, the poet, were for the King, but their cousin, Francis Godolphin of Treveneague, was a Parliamentarian ". On the other hand, it would seem to be a mistake to regard the two parties as " fairly evenly matched when war was declared " ; in these latter cases, if you observe, it was the junior branch of the family, without lands and influence, that espoused the cause of the Parliament, and the balance of the old families, with all the pull of their name and possessions, was unmistakably on the side of the King.

The great achievement of Cornwall in the Civil War was the creation of the Cornish Army, which, under Grenville and Hopton, fought the campaign of 1643 with unsurpassed heroism. At the very beginning, before men began to realise what war was, they found it hard to take it seriously ; as Hopton wrote, they were " so transported with the jollity of the thing that noe man was capable of the labour, care and discipline ". But as they became inured to war, the Cornish troops proved themselves to be of the first fighting quality. Their valour and discipline conquered the heart of Major Chudleigh, the ablest Parliamentarian officer in the West — " I never saw any army freer from vice nor more religiously inclined than I perceive the whole genius of this Army to be " — and he came over to the King's cause. The army stood its first severe test at Braddock Down in January ; and afterwards it went on from victory to victory, from Stamford Hill by Stratton to Lansdown and Roundway Down by Devizes, into Somerset and Wiltshire, to play the decisive part in Rupert's siege of Bristol, the King's greatest capture in the whole war. But it suffercd terribly ; the Cornish troops utterly wore themselves out in that campaign, but particularly at Lansdown in Bevil Grenville's charge straight up the hill against Waller's entrenchments, and at Bristol where they bore the brunt of the attack against the south-western ramparts of the city, with ladders that were too short to scale the walls, and so were driven back with one-third of their men dead. This was the end of the Cornish Army as such ; it had lost some two-thirds of its men and all its leaders. Things were never the same in the West ; spring had gone out of the morning, that spring when Francis Basset could write home to his wife at the Mount, after the happy victory at Stratton :

Dearest Soule, Oh Deare Soule, prayes God everlastingly. Reede ye inclosed. Ring out yor Bells. Rayse Bonefyers, publish these Joyfull Tydings, Beleeve these truthes. Thy own ffrs Bassett 6 o'clock ready to march.

The loss of their leaders, Grenville and Godolphin, Trevanion and Slanning, " the four wheels of Charles's wain " as the distich called them, was irreparable ; as Joseph Jane notes, it cast " a general damp upon the people, as that though they reteyned their loyaltie, they lost much of that life which appeared in their first actions ".

Sidney Godolphin had been killed early on, in February, in a skirmish at Chagford, " by an undiscerned and an undiscerning hand ", to quote Thomas Hobbes' famous phrase on the death of his friend. If Sir Bevil Grenville was both a more important and more popular figure to the army in general, the memory of Sidney Godolphin stood for another side to the war, one that is not less appealing and perhaps more rare. Like Falkland, whose friend he was, he had not wanted the war : " When the cards are shuffled no man knows what the game will be ", he had warned the House of Commons in his last speech ; whereas Grenville took by instinct to the war ; it was in his blood — " Thy Grandsire fills the Seas, and Thou the Land ", a poet wrote upon his death, recalling the glorious memory of the last fight of the *Revenge*. Godolphin was of a different temperament, a more complex nature ; a poet, he was of an extreme sensitiveness, a " wit " — by which we should mean an " intellectual " — and of a disposition that was both ardent and yet rested upon a foundation of melancholy. It may be that there was much of Cornwall in his nature — if we recall that very remarkable maxim of La Rochefoucauld : " L'accent du pays où l'on est né demeure dans l'esprit et dans le cœur, comme dans le langage " ; for the most distinguished Cornishmen there have been have often revealed the same combination. There was something more in Sidney Godolphin ; a man of intellectual power, the companion of Falkland and Hobbes, he was at bottom a religious mystic :

> Wise men in tracing Natures lawes,
> Ascend unto the highest cause ;
> Shepheards with humble fearefulnesse
> Walke safely, though their hight be lesse ;
> Though wise men better know the way,
> It seems noe honest heart can stray.
>
> There is noe merrit in the wise
> But love (the shepheards sacrifice).
> Wise men all wayes of knowledge past,
> To the shepheards wonder come at last :
> To know can only wonder breed,
> And not to know, is wonders seede.

In 1644 the main part of the whole southern campaign was fought out in Cornwall. Essex had, somewhat vaguely, allowed himself to be led on into the dangerous ground of the loyal peninsula ; detractors of the Presbyterians, like Ludlow, insinuated that he had been over-persuaded by Lord Robartes, who wished to " give himself an opportunity to collect his rents in those parts ". But Essex's uncertain purpose was itself a tribute to the importance of Cornwall to the Royalist cause — it was a keystone in the system ; for the export of tin financed the import of munitions, and the Cornish ports kept open the communications with France. The Parliamentarian advance gave Charles the opportunity for his best stroke in the war. Leaving Oxford, he followed Essex swiftly into the West ; the presence of the King in their midst roused all the resources of Cornish loyalty, while the primitive instinct of the people to defend their soil against the invading Parliamentarian army led them to rise *en masse*, to harry the fringes of the army and cut off their supplies. Shut in on all sides, in a hopeless tactical position, the Parliamentarian army of 6000 foot was forced to surrender ; and Charles, on leaving the county, was enabled to declare to Sir Francis Basset : " Now Mr. Sheriff, I leave Cornwall to you safe and sound." Five years later, at the trial of the King at Westminster, a young Cornishman gave evidence upon oath that " he did see the King marching in the head of his army about September 1644, a mile from Lostwithiel in Cornwall, in armour with a short coat over it unbuttoned . . . and that he saw him after that in St. Austell Downs drawing up his army ".

After 1644, the character of the war suffered a progressive degeneration. All its earlier gaiety and lightheartedness vanished ; it became sombre and ruthless. The Royalist command was paralysed by internal dissensions, which not even the presence of the Prince and his Council nor the responsibility for his safety could assuage. Sir Richard Grenville, who was in command, was a very different figure from his brother Bevil ; Miss Coate says well, " He was more like the Continental soldier of fortune : he had a cruel and malicious temper, a mocking tongue and an entire want of chivalry to a defeated opponent ". " Skellum Grenville " the Parliament always called him opprobriously and with consistency. The West was inexorably reduced, not less by the overwhelming weight of the Parliamentary forces than by its own exhaustion ; though there were not wanting gallant episodes, like the long resistance of Pendennis Castle under John Arundell of Trerice, old, diseased, and septuagenarian, who held out for months and then, writing at the bottom of the treaty of surrender " condescended unto by me John Arundell ", marched out with " Drums beating, Colours flying, Trumpets sounding ".

But indeed the resentment of the Cornish people for all that they had suffered in the war began to express itself as early as Skippon's retreat from Lostwithiel. Of 5000 foot that he set out with, only 1000 reached Poole ; the rest had been lost by sickness, death, desertion, or been cut off by the peasantry. Miss Coate puts it down to the " anger and cruelty which were the darker elements in the Cornish character ". But it must be remembered that Cornwall had suffered greatly not only from the slaughter of the 1643 campaign, for which not all the majesty of the royal letter of gratitude still hanging up in the Cornish churches could atone, but from the depredations of two armies fighting within its narrow compass in the next year. At the same time, the revenues from the mines, its main source of wealth, went into the royal coffers, while the county had the greatest difficulty in finding the £750 a week levied upon it as its quota towards the Royalist finances. No wonder the Cornish grew to resentment against the war and cooled in their attachment to the King's cause. It is in the exhaustion of its resources that the explanation is to be found for the comparatively easy submission of the county to Fairfax at the end.

Miss Coate rightly lays stress on a matter of funda-mental importance when she points out that government remained in the hands of the same class, the landed gentry, after the Civil War as before :

Thus the administration of Cornwall from 1646 to 1660 rested with the same class as under the Monarchy, and the Royalist was ruled by his equals, who preserved intact the Tudor tradition of unpaid service to the State. . . . From its inception in 1642 as the Militia Committee to its disappear-ance in 1660, the [Parliamentary] County Committee con-sisted mainly of the members of the leading county families. In 1643 the eleven members were all of the landed gentry ; in 1646, out of twenty-eight members, only one, William Ceely, merchant, was not of that class.

It is illuminating to trace how things settled down after the war in the Borough Accounts of a town like St. Ives.

Where, before, the Portreeve and his brethren were entertained at Christmas at Tehidy, the home of the Bassets, or at Godolphin — for instance, the Portreeve accounts in 1631, " Item, given by him att Godolphin att Christmas 5s. " — after the victory of the Parliament they went at Christmas to Clowance, to the St. Aubyns, who were Parliamentarians. But for all that, the bourgeois element was strengthened by that victory ; for if the landed class had been divided by the Civil War, the town oligarchies were fairly united in their allegiance to Parliament in the West as elsewhere, while Parliamentarian landed gentry, like the Robartes family, were still closely connected with the towns in which they had made their fortune.

It was the ecclesiastical condition of affairs during the Interregnum that revealed more clearly even than the financial side of things the temporariness of the Commonwealth and Protectorate. Larger issues, such as Cromwell's failure to root his military dictatorship in the foundation of the people's consent, showed up the insecurity of the whole régime. The obvious unsettledness and transitoriness of Church affairs in Cornwall revealed it no less. Notwithstanding that the County Committee spent £4000 on ministers from 1646 to 1649, people must have longed for the old settled order with the parson comfortably installed in his parish. No wonder there was such an outburst of joy at the Restoration ; the St. Ives accounts have a large expenditure on bell-ringing and feasting and ale-drinking in 1660. The King had come back to his own (this meant much in Cornwall, for did it not mean the visible return of the Duchy organisation ?) ; the old vicar returned to his parish, like Joseph Maye of St. Austell, who had gone back and tended his flock during the visitation of the plague, while the intruded parson had fled. And so the Royal Arms, which so frequently in Cornwall date from

Charles II, went up in the churches ; and men remembered the Royal Martyr and dedicated the new church at Falmouth to the sacred memory. In fact the country came back to Church and King as the secure foundation of social order, after a reign of the saints which ordinary mortals could not live up to, and of the Army which the finances of the country could not keep pace with.

Miss Coate concludes her book with the reflection that " the history of Cornwall in the seventeenth century is but the history of England in miniature, for everywhere is this dualism between the visible political changes at the centre and the unvarying life of the countryside, between the speculations of the few and the inarticulate conservatism of the many. Here then lies the function of the historian to appreciate both justly, for only by understanding the relation of the one to the other can the past be understood."

JOHN OPIE AND HARMONY COT [1]

Some years ago when I was on the north coast of Cornwall at Perranporth, recovering from illness, I made
a pilgrimage to Harmony Cot where John Opie was
born. He was, I think, the one Cornish painter of un-
disputed genius, and one of the more distinguished of
English painters. His career was a romance of successful
achievement. Starting from nothing, born in poverty,
with no one to teach him, with nothing but his own gifts
and that " energy of mind which men call genius ", as
Bernard Shaw puts it, with great determination and will-
power and hard work, Opie made himself a great artist,
one of the best painters of his day, and was buried in state
in St. Paul's Cathedral beside that other great West-
Country painter, Sir Joshua Reynolds.

Getting to Harmony Cot was quite an adventure, for
I was not yet steady on my legs, and it was a two-
mile walk up one of those valleys that run down to
the sea and meet at Perranporth. This one is called
Perran Combe ; and in the quiet of the summer evening,
taking my time, I followed the lane up through it : an
entrancing valley, very Cornish in character, with traces of
tin-streaming and little old tin-works all overgrown with
greenery now ; with close groups of Cornish elm, very
decorative and plume-like, and ash and young syca-
more growing, not much honeysuckle left — there had
been a lot — but plenty of earth-nut, cow-parsley, and
innumerable wild flowers I didn't know the names of.
Then at the end of the valley, uphill towards St. Agnes,
there is the hamlet of Trevellas, with Harmony Cot a little
way up on the right.

Opie was born in the middle one of a row of three

[1] Written in 1938.

whitewashed and thatched cottages, now all one house, with a fine screen of tall elms and a well-kept grass border before it. I stopped at the garden gate and leaned over : there was, very appropriately, a laurel bush growing over it, I noticed. Within, it was a typical Cornish cottage garden with fine ferns growing in profusion, honeysuckle, fuchsia, and rambler-roses growing over the doors. I felt as if I were the first person to have tracked down the house, all was so perfect and what one might have hoped — though there must have been many people who had been here before.

Presently an old gentleman came out and talked to me about the Opies. He was the last representative of the family, himself a bachelor, descended, I think, from Opie's brother ; for the painter had no children. He told me a number of things about the family ; that Opie's father came down from the parish of Egloshayle. " They were carpenters, and mine-carpenters at that," he said. " They got well-to-do, and then afterwards they got poor " — all this he told me with extraordinary melancholy, his voice going downhill as the Cornish voice does when referring to poverty.

I could see the whole picture in his words : the great growth of mining activity in this district nearly two hundred years ago brought them down here, provided work for a time, and when it slackened off there was nothing for them to do. Hence the poverty which surrounded Opie's childhood and hardened his fibre, his whole outlook. There was a certain pessimism which underlay his temperament ; in that he was not unrepresentative of the Cornish, though his mental energy burned with a fierce ardour from the first.

He was for ever drawing in crayons and chalks when a boy, in face of the active discouragement of his father, who wanted to make him a good carpenter. " The boy was good for nothin'," he said : " he was always gazin' upon cats, and starin' volks in the faace." Nothing, of course, could have been more suitable training for the lad's vocation ; and it is worth noting that his great strength as a painter later on was his realism, his absolute fidelity to what he saw in nature, when the more fashionable painters of the time were engaged in dressing up their subjects and making them more romantic and poetical. Opie in this matter was, I like to think, more akin to the French school of painters.

His father was always putting difficulties and obstacles in his way, to discourage him from his passion for drawing ; and many are the stories that are told of him as a lad : how as a boy of ten he began with the boast " I think I can draa a buttervlee as well as Mark Oates " — and did. And how, when a little later he was paid 5s. for copying a picture at Mithian farm, he ran about the house shouting, " I'm set up for life ! I'm set up for life ! " His father said, " That boy'll come to hangin', sure as a gun ".

But Opie had one great stroke of luck. The lad was noticed by Dr. Wolcot, himself a man of parts — he became celebrated afterwards as " Peter Pindar ", a satirist and writer of political verse. Wolcot took Opie to Truro to live with him for some time, taught him all he could about painting, sent him round the county to execute commissions for portraits and to paint subjects from the life, and at length when he thought the raw, uncouth young man was ready, took him to London and launched him on the precarious career of a portrait painter.

In London Opie was an immediate success. The fame of the untutored Cornish youth spread ; it became rather the thing to have your portrait painted by him ; commissions poured in ; it was said that during the season Orange Court outside his lodgings was blocked with the carriages of the fashionable waiting for sittings. Wolcot was an excellent chief of staff, who knew how to make the most of Opie's reputation for rudeness. He got him presented to George III and his Queen, who bought two of his pictures and gave him a commission. But all this success didn't in the least turn his head — it was much too solidly placed on his shoulders. It had the effect rather of driving him into himself. He was determined to preserve his aesthetic conscience, not to flatter his sitters, but to paint what he saw. "Shan't I draa ye as ye be?" he said to one of his fashionable ladies who wanted to be made into a romantic creation. In these early years he spoke broad Cornish, and he always retained a strong Cornish accent. He became noted for a caustic turn of wit, a very effective mode of defence with which he protected his sensitiveness. When someone asked him what he mixed his colours with, he replied "With brains, sir." One day when walking past St. Martin-in-the-Fields with Godwin, who was an unbeliever, the latter remarked that he was baptized there. "Curious," said Opie, who had divorced his first wife, "for I was married there. It's a poor shop, their work don't last."

When the first craze had died down for the "Cornish Wonder", as he was called, Opie had more time to settle down and develop his powers. He was determined to be, not merely a success, but, if he could, a really great painter. That almost despairing feeling, half hope, half despair, which all true artists feel, about ever reaching the best, drove him relentlessly on. In his twenty-five years of painting — he died when he was only forty-six — he painted between 750 and 1000 pictures. It was too much. He would have been a greater painter if he hadn't worked so hard, had let himself lie fallow for a bit. But he could not. He was practically self-taught, though for ever learning from the practice of his art. He made himself a man of reading and reflection too. His brother painter, Northcote, a fellow West-Countryman from

Plymouth, paid a tribute to Opie's conversation : " I always learn something new and original from him," he said.

Opie had the satisfaction of fulfilling himself in his art : though not old when he died, he had attained complete self-expression. In spite of, or rather I should say because of, his realism, through his integrity he reached in his best portraits a moving vision of what our life is : the pictures speak to us of its transitoriness, the mutability of human appearances. He succeeded in catching the moment on the wing, and fixing it for succeeding generations to enjoy : which is what all good art achieves. If you want to see his work at its best, look at the beautiful portrait of his mother in the Tate Gallery, painted with absolute truth and sympathy : an old wrinkled Cornish woman with bonnet tied under her chin, her large work-worn hands holding open the Bible before her. Or look at his self-portrait in the National Gallery, which is among his best : it is always interesting to see how an artist thinks of himself. If you are ever in Truro, step into the delightful little County Museum there, where they have three or four of the best Opies.

His living representative and I talked of these and many other matters over the garden gate that evening. I can't tell you all that he said now, except to transmit to you the extraordinary impression I got of the end of a family. " When my cousin and me are laid under the turf," he said, " all the Opies will be gone then." It was a melancholy reflection, like a theme out of Thomas Hardy. But even stronger was the impression I got of the place. It was virtually unchanged : the road, the hedges, the little sycamores, the valley, the cottages themselves. If Opie came back today, I thought, it would all be very recognisable. The impression of his presence was at its strongest in the lane up which I walked to join the main road from St. Agnes. I passed by the little chapel, almost old enough for him to have attended. The lane was thick with sloe bushes and brambles, a regular Cornish lane leading up to the desolate plateau where all the mines were, with ruined engine-houses standing out upon the cliffs towards the sea. How often Opie as a young lad must have gone up and down this lane, looked over this gate and across the fields to the valley and the hills beyond! The impression that genius attaches to the place it has once inhabited is extraordinary: it makes it its own; but never more so than in the case of this valley and the deserted mine-workings around Harmony Cot. In that quiet evening hour, is it surprising that I felt that I had come into contact in some indefinable way with that long-dead Cornish lad of genius?

KILVERT IN CORNWALL

LAST year there came to light a charming literary discovery, which has a distinct interest for Cornish people and all who want to know what our county looked like in the last century. It was the diary of a young Victorian clergyman : some twenty-two note-books of it, of which we are given a selection from the first eight in this volume.[1] The Rev. Francis Kilvert was a West-Countryman, who came of an old Wiltshire family ; but during the years covered by the diary he was a curate in Wales, at Clyro in Radnorshire, and the diary deals chiefly with life there. It is a fascinating picture of country life in the seventies in a remote district, as remote as Cornwall, that he gives. Kilvert was obviously a man of much charm, and he lived an active social life, very much welcomed at all the country houses around. But his position as parson opened all doors to him, and his diary is just as illuminating of the life of simple country folk, the villagers, the farmers, and their labourers, the shepherds out on the mountains. He was no less an observer of nature ; he had an astonishing eye for beauty, whether of landscape or in men and women, and, what is rarer, the gift of expressing what he saw precisely in words.

My one regret is that Kilvert wasn't curate of a Cornish parish, say Luxulyan, or St. Neot's, or St. Agnes. What a wonderful picture we should have had of Cornish life in the seventies ! But we have what is the next best thing, a careful record of his visit to Cornwall, with excursions all over the county, impressions of places and people, of his Cornish acquaintance, and, above all, of his friends the Hockins of Perran-ar-Worthal.

He came down in July 1870, the summer that the

[1] *Kilvert's Diary*, vol. i. Edited by William Plomer. (Cape, 1938.)

Franco-German War broke out ; never was the English countryside more peaceful or more prosperous. It was but a few years before the agricultural depression of the later seventies involved landowner, farmer, and labourer in common trouble. His impression of the first few miles of Cornwall was that the country was " bleak, barren, and uninteresting, the most striking feature being the innumerable mine works of lead, tin, and copper crowning the hills with their tall chimney shafts and ugly, white, dreary buildings or nestling in a deep, narrow valley, defiling and poisoning the streams with the white tin washing ". That takes us back to the years when the mines were still at their height ; but a short time and they were to close down and the great emigration from the county begin. Those later seventies must have been a hard time for Cornwall ! A little further down the line Kilvert notes that the country soon grew prettier. He was much impressed by the great timber viaducts crossing the ravines " at a ghastly height in the air " — the spider-bridges which were such a feature of Cornwall and such a decoration to our landscape. Many people must remember them : they have only recently vanished from their last hold, the line from Truro to Falmouth.

Kilvert calls his arrival at Tullimaar " the fulfilment of two years' dream ", so that he must have known his friends, the Hockins, for at least that time. He was on intimate, indeed affectionate terms with them, and it would be interesting to know if any of the family remembers the young, attractive clergyman with the full beard and lively fine eyes that observed everything, who has enshrined them so charmingly in his diary. He was evidently fond of them ; and a very good time they gave him in that hospitable house. Nor were they hospitable only to fellow human beings. Mrs. Hockin, he writes, " has two pet toads, which live together in a deep hole in the bottom of a stump of an old tree. She feeds them with

bread crumbs when they are at home, and they make a
funny little plaintive squeaking noise when she calls them.
Sometimes they are from home, especially in the evenings.
In the kitchen live a pair of doves in a large cage, and the
house is filled with their soft, sweet, deep cooing." Tullimaar is an attractive spot, looking across the woods of
Carclew and down Restronguet Creek ; and Kilvert gives
us an enchanting picture of the place in its best summer
colours, " the rich mingling of the purple beech tints with
the bright green of the other trees about the lawns and
shrubberies ".

Next day they went into Truro and down the river to
Falmouth. It was market day at Truro ; a market day
in the seventies, before ever the Cathedral was built.
What a pleasant picture of the old market he conjures
up ! He notes that the road was lively with market folk
and evidently we made a good impression on him :
" The Cornish people seem fine tall folk, especially the
women, much taller, larger people than the Welsh, and
most of them appear to be dark-haired ". He and Mrs.
Hockin went marketing together, and, of course, they
bought some pasties for lunch. While waiting on the
quay they watched an old invalid man from the infirmary
being very tenderly helped by two or three men into the
stern of a boat. Dear Mrs. Hockin told Kilvert that
" the Cornish are very kind and neighbourly to each
other, especially when they are in trouble ".

It was a blazing hot day for their excursion. They
embarked on the ebb-tide and " dropped down the river
with oars and mizzen sail between the steaming mud-
banks and sand flats, leaving Truro town in a dim blaze of
heat. Danish and Norwegian ships, three-masted vessels
from 200 to 400 tons, were lying anchored lower down
the river above, below Malpas." They went ashore at
Malpas to get ginger-beer at the inn for their picnic.
The boatman there was a regular character, a strong

temperance man and equally dry-humoured. He let out
at the Lord Falmouth of his day for shutting up his park
and not allowing any picnics in his woods. However, the
old boatman said he was determined to land picnic
parties on the estate whenever he chose and whatever
Lord Falmouth might say.

They went on down the river, a dead wind from the
south against them. They noted the oyster dredgers at
work, the old guard-ship, *Ganges*, in the river, " an old-
fashioned two-decker with the tall, elegant masts and
tapering spars, which one misses so much in the iron-
clads, and the long white bands checked with the black
squares of the portholes ". The works upon the harbour
at Falmouth had been left uncompleted, and looked rather
forlorn. At the station on their way back they ran into a
ship-wrecked crew : a grain ship from Odessa had run
upon the Stag's Horns Rocks, off the Lizard, in a dense
fog the morning before. The crew were fortunately all
saved, and here they were having a tremendous bust-up
with the railway porters about their belongings — all they
had saved from the wreck and upon which they were being
surcharged for excess luggage.

Next day they made a trip through the mining district
to Hayle, Kilvert greatly impressed : " Thou art Lord
of the world-bright tin ", he quotes from the old miners'
song. At St. Ives the Vicar told them that " the smell of
fish there is sometimes so terrific as to stop the church
clock ". Those were evidently the good old days when
tremendous catches of pilchards were landed at St. Ives.
While they were enjoying themselves on the beach, all
unknown to them, " a poor miner, who had gone out to
bathe in his dinner hour, was drowning in the bay very
near us ". From St. Ives they went on to St. Michael's
Mount ; but this, along with several other excursions later,
to Tintagel and so on, is omitted. To Cornish readers this
is rather a pity.

On Friday July 22nd, the Misses Emily and Charlotte Hockin came over from Truro, and they all started off for the Lizard " in a nice, roomy waggonette, large enough to carry 10 people, drawn by a pair of gallant greys ". At Gweek they " stopped to lunch by a hedge-side and brook while one of the horses, who had cast a shoe just before, was being shod " — one of the joys of the pre-motor age. At Mullion they drove to the Old Inn, kept then by Mary Mundy, " a genuine Cornish Celt, and a good specimen of one, impulsive, warm-hearted, excitable, demonstrative, imaginative, eloquent ". There follows one of the lovely descriptive sentences so typical of Kilvert and that deserve to make his fortune : " The window looked out over a waving field of reddening wheat which grew close up to the cottage wall, and the swaying ears of which were not far below the window sill ". The ladies of the party got lost on the cliffs and arrived late and exhausted for dinner. We may be sure that at these picnics all was very decorous and sedate and Victorian ; but not without fun.

The life and soul of the later parties seems to have been Captain Parker, then living at Rosewarne, who appears as a very hospitable, good-natured sort, full of jokes and facetiousness. He and his wife joined the Hockins for a grand excursion to Land's End on July 27th, of which Kilvert gives us a long and amusing account. They were all in high good spirits and Captain Parker " kept the waggonette in a roar ". They stopped on the way from Penzance to have sherry all round, and again at the inn near the Logan Rock for ale and cider. They certainly did themselves well on these picnics ; they always seem to be packing and unpacking the hampers. And Kilvert usually tells us what they had to eat ; quite rightly, for food is, perhaps, the most important thing about a picnic, almost as much as the company, and where you are going to only comes last. However, these were perfect picnics where all three were in tune : the party got on well together, the places they went to were such as only Cornwall can offer, the food was excellent. At Godrevy on another excursion we hear of grapes and claret on a grassy bank, dinner at Rosewarne and " a most admirable conger eel ", and home to hot supper at midnight off roast fowl. At Gurnard's Head on another day, Kilvert " actually ate and liked slices of melon, and, like Oliver Twist, asked for ' more '. Memorable day. How do all the ghosts of those rejected melons now rise up and accuse me ! " It is odd how these clerical diarists are so interested in food, though Kilvert has no more than a healthy interest and comes nowhere near the standards of Parson Woodforde.

But we haven't yet finished with the Land's End picnic. They went to see the Logan Rock, and on their way back ran into " a rude vulgar crew of tourists (real British) going down to the cliffs, grinning like dogs ; and one of the male beasts said in a loud, insolent voice, evidently meant for us to hear, ' I hope they haven't upset the Logan Rock '. For a moment I devoutly wished that we had." It seems a harmless enough remark, but evidently Kilvert's genteel party did not like the presence or the manners of the ordinary tripper, for there is another outburst later on against " the noisy rabble of tourists, males and females, rushing down the rocks towards Land's End, as if they meant to break their necks, and no great loss, either ". One knows so well that feeling ; the militant Captain Parker " suggested that a kicking might tend to mend their manners ". How well that gives us the feelings of the genteel towards the *profanum vulgus* of those days — the early days of popular tourism. With one touch of the pen Kilvert makes us see the place as it was on that hot summer day so many years ago : " The village was a paradise of black pigs which lay about in the glare of the sun under the hot granite walls, parroasted, but in great content ". What a descriptive gift he had and how he noticed everything !

He was greatly taken with Penzance, and reports a current saying that " the Penzance people and especially the women are said to be the handsomest in Cornwall ". I had never heard this before ; it would be interesting to know if it is still current.

One day they went down to Falmouth for the regatta. " A fresh breeze roughened the harbour, and the Roads were full of white horses coming in from the sea." How lovely ! it is like a Boudin picture, so gay and fresh in colour. " The town was very lively, stirring music of fifes and drums, all the Falmouth people out upon the narrow winding streets in their best clothes and gayest colours, the streets thronged with crowds marching along with the fifes and drums, and the town crier, a tall, grey bearded man in semi-uniform and high hat, stalked in solitary majesty with his bell making proclamation that at 1, 3, 5, and 7 o'clock the steam-boat *Pendennis* would make the tour of the harbour, taking people to see the regatta and the different points of interest round the harbour."

I suppose there are people in Falmouth still who remember that old town-crier, majestic figure, and the steam-boat *Pendennis*, and all the fun and gaiety of those days. They had reason to be gay, they inhabited a safer world than ours. That Falmouth entry reminds me of similar passages in the early diary of Charles Henderson when he was a boy living at Falmouth, which I hope will be published some day.

Another day and another picnic down the river at Tregothnan, " two boatloads of us, the hostess very nervous and fearful lest both boats should go to the bottom ". They walked up through the woods to St. Michael Penkivel Church, only just restored by Lord Falmouth " at a great expense " — would that he had spent less on it ! After tea, during which there was a great deal of fun that Kilvert reports with a gentle clerical humour, the young ladies rowed them across the river to Old Kea tower. For the first time one gets a glimpse into Kilvert's personal reactions, behind the screen of external politeness : " Young lady affectations, peculiarities, vagaries, etc., etc., unintelligible ", he notes briefly : not the first time that a young man has found them so : something had evidently annoyed him.

Next day an expedition to Gurnard's Head with the Parkers. A large omnibus and pair to take them ; but the hills took it out of the horses, " all abroad scrambling and staggering all over the place ", and a tyre almost came off and had to be tinkered on again. They arrived, however, at Zennor, " the strange old town in the granite wilderness in a hollow of the wild hillside, a corner and end of the world, desolate, solitary, bare, dreary, the cluster of white and grey houses round the massive old granite church tower, a sort of place that might have been quite lately discovered and where ' fragments of forgotten peoples might dwell ' ". After dinner they all went out to the Head. " Oh, that sunny, happy evening, gathering ferns among the cliffs. *Asplenium Marinum*, with its bright glossy green leaves, hiding itself so provokingly in the narrowest crevices of the rocks. I wandered round the cliffs to the broken rocks at the farthest point of the Head, and sat alone amongst the wilderness of broken, shattered, tumbled cliffs, listening to the booming and breaking of the waves below and watching the flying skirts of the showers of spray. Perfect solitude. The rest of the party were climbing about in the rocks somewhere overhead, but not a voice or sound was to be heard except the boom of the sea and the crying of the white-winged gulls. Not a sign or a vestige of any other living thing."

A further touch of personal feeling : Kilvert scrambled up the rocks to search for ferns for Mrs. Hockin. He was not very successful and her husband had got her some much finer ones, " but she did not despise mine, though they were very poor little ones in comparison ".

They got back to hot supper at Rosewarne at midnight : " the dining room at Rosewarne beautifully hung round with horns, antelope, stag, gnu, buffalo, etc." They didn't get home to Tullimaar till three in the morning. " As we passed down the creekside the masts of a vessel showed against the sky. A sailing lighter had come up the creek at high tide with a load of limestone and was lying at the quay waiting to unload and go down again with the next tide. . . . This morning we met two girls smartly dressed, and driving cows to market with parasols up."

After such late junketings they spent the next few days quietly at home, Kilvert reading Bottrell's *Traditions and Hearthside Stories of West Cornwall*, on the garden seat under the ilex upon the lawn. He was interested to find so " many words, ideas and superstititions and customs kindred to those of Wales ". He copies down a verse of the old miners' song :

> Here's to the devil
> With his spade and wooden shovel,
> Digging tin by the bushel
> With his tail cocked up.

Mrs. Hockin brought out her copy of Tennyson's *Idylls of the King* with the Doré illustrations. In the afternoons they sat together under the copper beech looking through photograph albums, and in the evening music and singing in the drawing-room after dinner.

On August 5th they went for their last excursion to Godrevy, Kilvert already in the unhappy, nostalgic mood one knows so well when about to leave a place where one has been happy. They called at Rosewarne and at Gwythian to see the remains of the British church there buried in the sand. Kilvert comments sadly, " Within the memory of persons still living, the altar was standing, but the place has got into the hands of a dissenting farmer who keeps the place for a cattleyard and sheepfold and what more need be said ". Kilvert took " a great fancy to this village by the sea, with its nice church and schools ; but the curate complained a good deal about the people and their ineradicable tendency to dissent ".

They had a good day at Godrevy and Kilvert was delighted by the sight of a seal swimming and basking not fifty yards from the shore. At the end of the day, he notes : " The last longing, hungering farewell look at the Cornish sea. The white sand towans of Phillack. Lelant Church, among the sand. St. Ives and the great bay, the crest of St. Michael's Mount, the Portreath lighthouse and Trevose Head, so exquisitely clear was the air."

Next morning Kilvert was up early packing and rushing down the Truro drive " to get some sprays from the bush of white heather. The trees were all dripping from early showers, the tears of the morning. The morning was fresh, cool and lovely, and the beautiful place looked more beautiful than ever." In spite of all, he missed the train at Truro and so had one more morning at Tullimaar. " Mrs. H. was planting ferns, the Gurnard's Head Asplenium in the potting house, and I leaned on the window-sill outside watching her and making her laugh with Cowper's ' Killing Time ', ' The Parson merry is and blithe ', etc. The second parting. And so endeth a very happy time."

Kilvert was desolate at leaving Cornwall : it is evident that he had quite lost his heart to it ; and no wonder, for it was Cornwall at its loveliest then, not yet spoiled. When he got back to his father's rectory, Langley Burrell in Wiltshire, that night he poured out his soul to his diary in the way one does. " The desolate misery," he writes, " the acute agony of those first four terrible hours, and the cold, heavy, dull pain of the rest of the long nine hours' journey as we flew through all the length of the three Western Shires. How different from the journey down. A bitter moment when the Tamar was crossed and Cornwall left behind, perhaps for ever. All the bright memories and names of the places (now so dear) together visited, crowding up. The wild, restless longing, the hopeless yearning, the gnawing hunger of regret."

But it was not only to the place that Kilvert had lost his heart, there was someone whom he was leaving behind. We can all recognise the language : " All through the journey my eyes were perpetually seeking for the one familiar face and form which have been so constantly before them for the last three weeks, seeking, seeking, baffled, longing, all in vain. ' The further that thou fliest now so far am I behind.' And the wretchedness, the utter misery, of the blank and continual disappointment. ' He saw many faces, but there was no St. Clare.' The name and scene of Godrevy with all its dear memories dwelt especially in my mind and almost moved me to tears. I seemed to linger once more over the last fond look at the Cornish sea. And in what company. I seemed to see again the buried church, the ancient British church in Gwythian Sands, the white lighthouse, the spray on the rocks, the heaving bar, the sunny steeps, the cliffs, the seals, St. Ives, the bellbuoy, the great fig tree in Gwythian Churchyard, the rocks where poor Drury was lost on Palm Sunday, the distant view of dear Portreath, and the name kept on coming up, Godrevy, Godrevy. With a mournful cadence, Godrevy, farewell. Unknown till yesterday. But now how dear, a possession for ever. And now a thing of the past, drifting hourly further away. Farewell. Farewell. I thought — was it so — that there were tears in those blue eyes when we parted. I know there were tears in mine. Forget me not, oh, forget me not."

Kilvert was a sensitive creature, extraordinarily susceptible to the charm of women; moreover, he was a poet, and knew how to express what he felt. Need we be surprised that he had quite lost his heart to the charming young Mrs. Hockin?

Nor did he forget Cornwall and his friends there. When he got back to his curacy in Wales and went to Hay Flower Show, " an *Asplenium Marinum* carried me back to dear Gurnard's Head, and for the moment I forgot the show and people and everything else ". One night he dreamed of Gwythian and that he was married not to the fair Mrs. H., but to Mrs. Danzey who, I suppose, was his housekeeper. It made him wake up in a cold sweat. But his satisfactions were purely vicarious. In February of next year a daughter was born to the Hockins — Kilvert pasted a cutting from *The Times* announcing it into his diary; and they wrote asking him to become godfather to the child. " I wrote at once to tell him how glad I shall be to do as they wish. It was the thing I had been longing for. Now I shall have a real right in the child. Silver and gold have I none and I cannot give her valuable presents, but such as I have she shall have, and what I can do for her, with God's help, shall be done."

Later in the year, in August, when he was at Langley Burrell again, one afternoon when he was just beginning to write, " there was a ring at the bell and some people were shown into the drawing-room. . . . I went down and there were actually in the flesh the Hockins. She came quickly across the room and put her hand into mine. It seemed too good to be true. She was looking so nice and well and young and pretty, and they were delighted to come to the old village again. They had come up to Warminster to look at a house . . . as they have sold Tullimaar."

Next morning after breakfast he went down to watch for them across the common and homefield. " Soon her white dress glinted through the trees and she was carrying a scarlet cloak. We spent a happy two hours sitting under the acacia and wandering about the lawn talking. We gathered for them what apricots we could find ripe and at 11.45 the fly with their luggage came from Langley Green to take them to the station. We drove down to the station in the pony carriage to see them off, and I sent many kisses by her mother to my little godchild Beatrice. Their visit was like a gleam of sunshine but it was sad and melancholy after they were gone."

And so, on this Cornish note, the first volume ends.

In the second volume [1] we hear more about the Hockins, and even a little more about Cornwall, though Kilvert never came here again : his friends left Tullimaar and went to live near his home, at Taunton. One day Hockin told Kilvert an amusing story of a happening in St. Michael Penkivel Church — just the sort of fantastic thing that is liable to happen in a Cornish church or to the Cornish clergy. It apparently referred to the Hockins' predecessor at Tullimaar, a Mr. Lanyon. "He had money and other troubles and went out of his mind. Unfortunately the outbreak happened in church. He was living in Falmouth and one Sunday morning he went to Tregothnan Church. During the celebration of the Communion Lanyon went to the desk and began reading the Litany aloud. The curate came down to the Chancel and asked him to desist. Lanyon turned on the curate. ' Get thee behind me, Satan,' he said severely, and went on reading the Litany aloud. The curate went behind him and returned to the Altar. The Rector now came down and remonstrated with Lanyon. Lanyon made no answer but took up the great Prayer Book and knocked the Rector on the head."

Next year, in September, Kilvert went to visit the Hockins at Taunton, and found that " many things about

[1] Published 1939.

the house and place within and without reminded me strongly of Tullimaar ". On leaving, " Mrs. Hockin gave me what I valued extremely, one of the plants of *Asplenium Marinum* fern which I got for her at Gurnard's Head two years ago and which she has kept ever since. She brought down to show me her husband's birthday present to her, a magnificent sealskin jacket trimmed deep with the loveliest soft grey-brown beaver's fur." In December he visited them again, this time to christen an infant. " It was pleasant to see dear Mrs. Hockin again, looking bright and merry and like her old self. She told me about her illness. It was almost desperate at one time, and the doctors said that nothing could have saved her but her youth and a splendid constitution."

The warmth, the concern of friendship were still there, and the memory of the emotion he had felt two years ago — but now it was a memory. There is something touching about that : it is so true of our human condition : the passion that once was so intense as hardly to be bearable, so absorbing as to exclude everything and give one the illusion of being eternal, is transmuted by time into something gentler — and one finds it is to the memory that one is being faithful. Kilvert went on one more visit to the Hockins, in September next year, and they made an excursion together to Lynton, where Kilvert made a characteristic entry in his diary, full of his own poetic sensibility : " I got up at 6 o'clock as the sun was rising behind the Tors. The house was silent and no one seemed to be about. I unlocked the door and let myself out into the garden. It was one of the loveliest mornings that ever dawned upon this world. A heavy dew had fallen in the night and as I wandered down the beautiful winding terraced walks every touch sent a shower from the great blue globes of the hydrangeas, and on every crimson fuchsia pendant flashed a diamond dew drop. The clear pure crisp air of the early morning blew fresh and exhilarating as the breeze came sweet from the sea. No one was astir, everything was silent, and I seemed to have the beautiful world to myself. The only sound that broke the stillness was the roaring of the Lynn far below. The scene which was clothed in darkness as we came in last night now lay suddenly revealed in the full splendour of the brilliant morning light, glowing with all its superb colouring, the red cliffs of the mighty Tors, the purple heather slopes and the rich brown wilderness of rusting fern, the snowy foam fringe chafing the feet of the cliffs, and the soft blue playing into green in the shoaling water of the bay where the morning was spread upon the sea.

" In the quiet early sunny morning it seemed to me as if that place must be one of the loveliest nooks in the Paradise of this world."

The world was indeed a paradise for a man who felt and could write about it like that. Those were the moments of revelation for which Kilvert lived : he was indeed at heart as much the pure aesthete as ever Proust was — or, for that matter, as William and Dorothy Wordsworth.

And that is the last that we hear of the Hockins. How much we should like to know what happened to them, what became of the attractive young wife who took Kilvert's heart that day when he got the *Asplenium Marinum* for her on Gurnard's Head, whose image haunted the compartment for him all the way back from Cornwall. Our curiosity is the measure of the spell that he lays on us ; his diary has all the veracity and the pathos of life. From now on the ways of the friends separated ; I hope it was no shadow that came between them, though it is a little strange that there is no mention whatever of his Cornish friends in the third and last volume of the diary.

Kilvert went back to the Welsh Border again, to become Rector of Bredwardine, not far from Clyro where he had been so happy. But a few years and he was dead, five weeks after his marriage, still young. He left for a memorial of himself this diary, which I think will not soon perish ; and from it we may call up that now distant summer in Cornwall, those delicious heat-haze days of the seventies, see the place as it looked to those loving observant eyes, hear again those long-vanished voices of his Cornish friends.

THE SENTIMENTAL JOURNEY

EVERY journey homeward is a sentimental journey. Or so, I fancy, it must be for anyone whose good fortune it is to journey homeward to Cornwall. At least, it always is for me : I know the ground so well by now, that I look forward to the familiar landmarks, so often observed before, here a hill or a wood, there a farmhouse or a pond, with a start of recognition, always with expectancy, and with a certain contented satisfaction when it has flashed by and been left behind.

What a curious angle it is from which to observe the slow motions of men's lives. It was Robert Louis Stevenson, I believe, who first had the courage to remark how good a way a railway journey was of seeing the country. But there is something more strange in it than that. For a moment one enjoys a swift intrusion into the quiet life that is proceding ; one breaks into its intimacy. The journey seems bounded by two dimensions, to be contained within the moving pictures upon the window-panes : a long ribbon of experience, thin and shallow, from which one infers the rest. There are the lives of simple plodding toil, of horses and of men ; the June hay is being gathered in, or the November plough team crosses the folds of the fields ; a white path strikes upwards from the valley to a ridge of the downs, and there is a single, purposeful figure patterned on the road, bent towards the summit.

How often one has noticed just such things ! And then, as the train draws on into the West, getting nearer and nearer home, one's attention quickens ; there is a subdued excitement in passing by the stations, and people come in bound for some Cornish haven, one wonders where. Just as conversely, in coming away from home, the attention remains on the stretch all the way to the

Tamar, and only when the boundary is crossed does one settle down to read, and to subdued observation. Perhaps it may be because of the sheer beauty of the line from Par onwards to the east that I always find this happening to me. Anyhow, there is no more exciting stretch of a railway journey that I know in this country; and only one that I have to admit abroad. That is the line from Munich to Vienna, which, I seem to remember, skirts the mountains and keeps them in sight all day. There they are, blue in the distance, irrefragable, unreal landscape of a dream. There is a stop at Salzburg, where the mountains come into the town; and where, in the silence around the train at a standstill, I once heard a lark (larks in the evening at Carn Grey, I thought!) singing loud above the streets.

But the present was no such journey by day, going through the familiar country and passing the accustomed places. For the first time I was travelling home by night, hurrying on a mission. I had come to the conclusion that I could not be anywhere else than at home in all this excitement; that I ought to be there now, for that was the place that my thoughts kept turning to at such a time.[1] Having decided at the last moment, here I was late at night at the station.

There were a few lights flickering in the draughts of the platform, and only one other traveller taking the midnight train. He was a young Swedish cadet, in uniform, fair, but dark-tanned; had come across the country from Dungeness, where he had landed a sick comrade from his ship, and was on his way to join it at Falmouth. No sign of a ticket office opening, and we were thrown together in dealing with the guard. This we did, helping each other out in German, which he spoke rather better than English. Together we watched a station cat clamber from the platform down to the rails: I, a little horrified

---

[1] Written at the time of the General Election in 1929.

to think of its danger, and the young Swede, to suggest that it would know its way about all right under the train, crouching his shoulders and making a stealthy motion forward with his hands. An expressive friendly gesture, endearing from one stranger to another ; and that was the last I saw of him.

Travelling by night in a sleeper was a new experience, and hard to settle into. Besides, I kept thinking of the purpose of my journey, half repenting, in the way one does, of having undertaken it, and yet knowing that it was my duty. And at last, all such thoughts were lulled to rest by the insistent rhythm of the wheels, beating out " Home again ! Home again ! " into the strange spaces of the night. So that when the guard came in the morning to wake me, bringing my tea, for we had already crossed the boundary and were in Cornwall, it seemed so short a time since I had left Oxford. And I thought of that other night journey, fit to be remembered by the side of this, coming back from Bavaria to England. All night long the train pulsed steadily across the highland and the plain ; and when morning came, there we were journeying along by the side of the Rhine, the river broad and like a dull mirror in the earliness ; the hillsides banked with terraces, and here and there a castle perched darkly on a crag in the distance.

That had seemed the most delectable of nights of travel. And yet, waking and finding Cornwall overnight around one was a more intimate sensation, and overwhelming. It was Lostwithiel again, so soon : there were the trees by the river, and I saying softly over them " O, lovely ! O, lovely ! " to the unawakened dawn. Here was a field of clover sloping steeply to a combe. The seeping mists were folded under the arms of the trees in the woods asleep.

To be home again : the trees are more lovely ; the fields greener, the gorse more golden ; the birds sing sweeter ; all the land is a dream.

OUR LOCAL HERITAGE

THE love for one's native place is, I believe, the foundation of all patriotism. It is only natural that wherever later in life we may wander, we should look back with affection to the first and smallest horizons of which we are conscious, the horizons of our childhood and of our home. For indeed it is our native place that holds the deepest meaning for us ; and we are all the luckier if we belong to a locality which possesses individuality, as almost any Cornish parish does. The modern world, and particularly certain classes of society in it, are only too full of cosmopolitans : people who are at home anywhere, which is the same thing as being at home nowhere. Most big towns, and especially the great capitals like London, Paris, Vienna, and Berlin, have a large floating population of mortals who seem to spend their time and energy in packing up to go on to the next place. For my part, though I feel that such people have the doubtful advantages of speaking three or four languages badly, instead of one well, they do not know the joy of caring for one place in the world more than anywhere else ; they are in the great misfortune of having no roots in the soil.

Those of us who are fortunate enough to feel that we belong to some especial spot on the English countryside, and particularly those whose roots are in the St. Austell district, to whom this little inquiry is dedicated,[1] have inherited in the town and its girdle of townships and villages a heritage which we alone can enjoy to the fullest. Now in what does it consist, it may be asked. It consists in the character of the place itself. And to my mind there are two ways in which that character is achieved. There

[1] Written for the *St. Austell Hospital Handbook, 1927.*

is first of all the material side of the thing, the actual streets and roads and lanes that were laid down in their roughest outlines in times so remote one can't be sure when. Isn't there a romance in the very roads we walk on ; who knows with what difficulties and amid what dangers the obscure straggling tracks were first made across the hills and the downs, and by the slopes into the valley, and along the marshes and the moors ? And then there are the buildings, gathered together in the course of centuries, and with infinite pains extended and rebuilt and changed. Think of the changes and chances which an old building like the Parish Church or the Market House has seen, compared with the short enough space of human life. The second and more difficult way in which the character of a place is built up is by the accretion of memories of the former generations who spent their lives there, and now lie quietly in the churchyard. Now and then some of them leave us records of their lives, and we can trace out their joys and sorrows as if they were our own ; for we can be sure they would wish to be remembered.

"I would not be forgotten in that place", wrote the poet, Robert Stephen Hawker, after a lifetime of devotion in his parish on the north coast of Cornwall, at Morwenstow. But the way of remembrance is the more difficult way, because the knowledge of the old days and the memories of the old people are borne in mind by only a few in each generation.

Sometimes I think that it is the melancholy privilege of those who have to spend much of their time away from home to be the better judges whether the changes made while they are away are an improvement to the common heritage. I am sure that we take the world, and the good things in it, too much for granted. Living every day in the midst of places and buildings that have been handed down to us from the past, we stand in need of a mind freshened by absence to point out that this curve of the street is individual and ought not to be spoiled, or that this old doorway or that bow-window with the small panes of glass is a thing of delight and should be preserved as part of the heritage for future generations, even if we are incapable of appreciating it ourselves.

How many good things there are in and around Fore Street, when we come to think of it ! Have you ever noticed how excellent is the front of that house with its high seventeenth-century gable and the porch with the fine dimensions ? [1] That house was, I believe, a dower-house of one of the old neighbouring families, the Tremaynes of Heligan. Or there is the fine family mansion of the eighteenth century, in Menacuddle Street, " so long and so honourably occupied by the Veale family ", as Canon Hammond notes—which now is a general stores. Or there is the Market House, standing solid and impressive, unbending before all the winds that blow, like the century in which it was built. Or again, there are the quiet houses standing a little way back from the street, across from the Public Rooms ; so unpretentious and retiring—like the domestic life of the early nineteenth century of which for me they are always an expression. And yet, just so were the houses in which all the quiet drama of Jane Austen's novels played itself out ; and when I think of Barrie's play on the same period, *Quality Street*, it always connects itself with those houses in my mind. And last, there is, what we may justly be proud of, the church : how many trouble themselves to appreciate all the history, all the record of human effort that has gone to make such a building ?

It has what is, all told, the finest of Cornish church towers ; even in Oxford, that city of spires and towers, there is only one, that of Magdalen, that is indubitably finer. What makes ours at St. Austell so remarkable is

[1] It has vanished since.

the splendid series of images carved on it, unbroken, un-decayed, unspoiled. On three sides — north, east, and south — there are the twelve apostles, four on each face. But it is to the west that the tower displays its crowning glory : the resplendent decorative grouping which begins on the lowest tier with three figures ; our Lord holding the pennon of the Resurrection ; on his right hand, a hermit in a sheepskin, on his left, a vested bishop : perhaps St. Austell himself and St. Mewan, whose inseparable disciple he was. The second tier displays the Annunciation : the Blessed Virgin on one side, the Angel Gabriel on the other, the vase with the flower of the Annunciation springing up between them. On the third tier, at the summit, is a representation of the Trinity (to whom the church was re-dedicated by Bishop Bronescombe in 1259) : God the Father with the crucified Son between his knees—the whole figure of the Father of such grave majesty that it is not too much to think of it as a masterpiece, the masterpiece of an unknown, unnamed West-Country sculptor of the fifteenth century. Perhaps — it is likely enough — he came down to us from Wells or Exeter. Anyhow, let us remember with pride that long-dead craftsman who left us such a thing of beauty. One of the finest things in the whole West Country — I dare say it is unique of its kind, and, though we who live in the place hardly give it a thought or a look, well worth a pilgrimage from far to see.

But there is another side to it all than this : there is the tide of life that has ebbed and flowed through these places and in these streets for generation after generation. The sense of this ceaseless movement, the reverence for the past, is the beginning of wisdom. We should treasure what little scraps of information there are to be gleaned. How John Wesley in passing through our town on one occasion thought it " a neat little town upon the side of a fruitful hill " ; and so, with his gift for phrases, fixed for ever the essential description of St. Austell in the seventeen-eighties. And how on another occasion (August 17th, 1789) he found the state of the street not all that it might be : " I knew not where to preach, the street being so dirty ". Perhaps this was the time when he preached from the steps of a house in Fore Street, as tradition tells ; but now, neither steps nor house is there.

And there are other memories : of the sprightly Miss Celia Fiennes who rode through England on a side saddle in the sixteen-nineties and left amusing descriptions of the state of local manners at that time ; of Ralph Allen, born at St. Blazey and immortalised in Fielding's *Tom Jones* ; of Samuel Drew, at once cobbler and metaphysician (I think as I write of the noble face with the hard, honourable lines and the luminous eyes of the portrait reproduced in Hammond's book; and the touching inscription after his life of toil, " The infirmities of 66 are coming on me ").

Among these old worthies there is a pleasant thing to report, that a recent researcher has been able to find a good deal of information about the most remarkable woman who comes into our history : Loveday Hambly, whose home at Tregangeeves was the centre and source of comfort for the early Quakers in the West of England.[1] Of all the gracious figures at a time in English history when nobility came more easily to men's character, the good Mistress of Tregangeeves appears as one of the most noble and most charitable, and of tried fortitude. A servant-boy of her household testified to the charity of her ways : " She was more like a mother to me than a mistress ; and her tables were always largely and bountifully spread ". Loveday Hambly was converted to the Friends late in middle life by her meeting with George Fox ; and thereafter endured much persecution and not infrequent imprisonment for her faith and for her refusal to pay tithe. In 1658 there is the somewhat humorous

---

[1] *Vide* L. V. Hodgkin's delightful *A Quaker Saint of Cornwall.*

note of a distress that was made against her "for refusing to pay 9s. towards the repairing of the Pope's old decayed Massehouse !" . . . And later there are frequent and more serious troubles. But through all the difficulties of this early period of Quakerism, Loveday remained a steadfast light for the Friends in the West. And when she came to die, and was buried in the quiet burying-ground on the brow of the hill as you go out of the town towards Truro, the reticent Quakers broke their habit of bare entries in their Register for the first and last time, to record the burial of " Loveday Hambly, long time famous for her hospitality and good works !"

The way in which the story of Loveday Hambly was almost forgotten, and then after the lapse of two hundred and fifty years has been brought back into the light again, shows how frail a thing is the local memory of the past. But we can do something to keep the old times and people in remembrance by showing an intelligent pride in our history, and encouraging its study by supporting such bodies as the Royal Institution of Cornwall and the Federation of Old Cornwall Societies, which have been the means of reviving interest in much that would otherwise have been lost.

And no less frail, unhappily, is the actual appearance of the town and its villages as we grew to know them. Changes must come, roads be made and houses built, we all know. But are we doing all we can do to ensure that the work of this generation is in keeping with the spirit of the old ? The place as we knew it was a place of original and individual aspect. Strangers came and admired its quaintness. The tendency of much recent addition has been to flatten St. Austell to the dull level of any other place. We gain little but lose a great deal by suburbanising our villages and changing the names of our places and streets. What we gain is to be one degree more like Surbiton ; what we lose is the infinite variety of old prospects, old manners, and old names.

Everything depends in this matter on the growth of an informed local opinion. We should learn to be ashamed when vulgar and tactless and showy houses, complete with cheap wood verandahs and coloured panes of glass in the windows, appear along the country lanes and spoil our views. As for building in prominent positions on the cliffs, the pride and glory of Cornwall, the thing should be placed beyond the pale by public opinion. And with names, too, we can do much to preserve our distinctive characteristics from being overwhelmed in the flood of ignorance and semi-education. What is better than the simple homespun names with their roots in the past and with their meanings, though hidden in our forgotten language : names like Polketh (spelt as it was pronounced), Treleaven's Cross, Watering Hill, Menacuddle Street ? There is poetry in names ; when we are touched by the names of flowers, it is the flowers of Shakespeare's England, as he tells them over in the Plays :

> The fairest flowers o' the season
> Are our carnations and streaked gilly flowers. . . .
> Here's flowers for you ;
> Hot lavender, mints, savory, marjoram . . .

The moral of it all is there. There is not so much beauty about us that we can afford to destroy it. And if we have been fortunate in our birth-place, and in a heritage of a distinctive character, we ought to do our duty in preserving it from despoilment. The responsibility is not only to ourselves and to later generations who may come to love our common home as we love it, but to the men and women in all parts of the world who have gone forth from home, yet who retain a living image of their native place and would not have it much changed.

THREE GREAT TRAVELLERS ON
ST. AUSTELL[1]

IN the previous essay I was concerned primarily with
the love of one's native place and for its heritage of
memories and beauty. That love, which is simple
enough when unrealised, is often a complex and sub-
jective affair ; for it becomes entangled in our minds with
our remembrance of childhood and all its associations of
peace and security. Our home town may in fact be no
more peaceful and secure than anywhere else ; indeed, I
can well imagine that some people, engaged in the dusty
cult of what is go-ahead and modern, would repudiate
the notion that we are restful and unhurrying, with
considerable warmth. And yet, when we turn for delight
and comfort to that image of home which every Cornishman carries round the world with him, we feel that we
are turning to a haven of quiet. It is because our own
locality means a great deal more to us than it may really
be in itself, or in the eyes of more objective observers
from outside ; and as we grow older we begin to understand, a little sadly, that what we are seeking is not only
the image of home, but the dream of vanished childhood.

But there is another way of devotion, which, though
less rare in quality, offers more results. We may not all
be equally good at searching after dreams ; but we can
at least build up a little information about our town and
its past. Having pursued for a time the path of knowledge, picking up a few scraps of local history here and
there, we may be surprised to find that we have passed
over the border of mere interest and entered upon a real
devotion of the heart.

If we want to get back in our minds to what St. Austell

[1] Written for the *St. Austell Hospital Handbook, 1928.*

was like in the past, there is hardly a better way than to read the accounts left of the place by travellers who passed through it in bygone times. We gather up their impressions, and at the same time use them as fuel for our own religion of place.

My three travellers, then, are John Leland, Miss Celia Fiennes, and John Wesley. Not that they are the only people who, passing through the town, left any record of it ; but because in their different ways they are the most interesting and the most representative. The three of them cover a large expanse of time — from the Reformation to that Industrial Revolution which created all that is most characteristic of the modern age ; yet in all that time from the middle of the sixteenth century to the end of the eighteenth, it is unlikely that the town changed as much as it has done within the memory of the oldest alive now. It is a refreshing thing, in an age of such changes and chances, to rest one's mind for a little on the eternal sameness of men's lives in the countryside and in the country towns throughout the ages ; men must have gained strength from that stability, I am sure.

> Along the cool sequester'd vale of life
> They kept the noiseless tenor of their way.

John Leland, who was appointed King's Antiquary by Henry VIII, was conducting his tours of England from 1534 to 1543 — the critical years of the Dissolution of the Monasteries. His chief end and aim was to collect information for a complete survey of all the antiquities, particularly documents, deposited over the face of the land. It was an impossible task ; Leland's collections were still far from complete when he became insane, and perhaps no wonder ! But in the course of his indefatigable journeying he collected notes which amount to an extraordinarily detailed and reliable topography of the whole country. And fortunately his notes on Cornwall are among the fullest he devoted to any county. The sentence or two he devoted to us are interesting as the starting point for all subsequent commentary upon our town and us. It is obvious that Leland was travelling up the county by way of Penryn, Truro, then down to St. Mawes and along the coast to Gerrans and the Dodman. There we get on to our own ground :

From Chapel Land to Pentowen a sandy bay, whither the fisher boats repair for succour, a 2 miles.

Here issueth out a pretty river that cometh from St. Austelles, about a 2 miles and half. And there is a bridge of stone of the name of the town. This river runneth under the west side of the hill that the tower of St. Austelles standeth on. At St. Austelles is nothing notable but the parish church. From Pentowen to Black Head about a mile. . . . And in the cliffs between the Black Head and Tywardreath Bay is a certain cave wherein appeareth things like images gilted. And also in the same cliffs be veins of metals, as copper and other.

I have modernised his spelling except for names ; otherwise his account would look unbelievable, in the complicated sixteenth-century style. But in whatever spelling, it is evident that the learned antiquary was much more interested in Tywardreath than in St. Austell ; and indeed, more in Fowey (he spells it very sensibly Faweye) than in Tywardreath. For while he was pleased at the fine tomb of the founder at the west end of Tywardreath Priory Church (of which, alas, nothing remains), he waxed really eloquent over the prosperity of Fowey, gained " partly by feats of war, partly by piracy ", and over the fine house of Place built by Thomas Treffry and " right fair and strong embattled . . . and unto this day it is the glory of the town building of Fowey ".

Miss Celia Fiennes is a very different matter and much more sprightly ; moreover, she gives St. Austell rather more attention than most other places in Cornwall. She was a sort of seventeenth-century blue-stocking, of very good Puritan family, who had the interesting notion of travelling over the length and breadth of the land for the sake of her health and the improvement of her conversation. From a reference during her Cornish tour to " the peace being newly entered into with the French ", I gather she was in the county in the year 1697 ; that being the year of the Peace of Ryswick, which brought a close to a period of nine years war. And later, she dates her visit to " the time of harvest, though later in the year than usual being the middle of September ". The poor lady managed to come into a patch of vicious autumn weather ; and in the condition of our roads she had a difficult and even hazardous journey down from Plymouth. However, she was a cheerful enough soul to draw amusement from her discomforts ; all the way from Looe to Fowey (unrecognisable as Loun and Hoile !) her horse was floundering in quagmires :

here my horse was quite down in one of these holes full of water but by the good hand of God's providence which has always been with me Even a present help in time of need, for giving him a good strap he fflounced up again though he had gotten quite down his head and all, yet did retrieve his feet and gott quite clear off the place with me on his Back. . . .

Well, to pass on, I went over some Little Heath Ground but mostly Lanes, and those stony and Dirty, 3 mile and half to Parr ; here I fferyd over again, not but when the tyde is out you may ford it.

Thence I went over the heath to St. Austin's wch is a little market town where I lay, but their houses are like barnes up to the top of the house. Here was a pretty good dining room and Chamber within it and very neate Country women. My Landlady brought me one of ye west Country tarts ; this was the first I met with though I had asked for them in many places in Sommerset and Devonshire ; its an apple pye with a Custard all on the top, its ye most acceptable entertainment it cd be made me. They scald their Creame and milk in most parts of those countries and so its a sort of Clouted Creame as we call it, with a little sugar and soe put on ye top of ye apple pye. I was much pleased with my supper tho' not with the Custom of the Country whch is a universall smoaking, both men, women and children have all their pipes of tobacco in their mouths and soe sit round the fire smoaking wch was not delightful to me when I went down to talk with my Landlady for information of any matter and Customs amongst them. I must say they are as Comely sort of women as I have seen anywhere tho' in ordinary dress — good black eyes and Crafty enough and very neat. Halfe a mile from hence they blow their tin which I went to see.

She then goes on to a long description of the working of the tin mines at Polgooth ; but for a discussion of this I would refer the reader to Mr. Hamilton Jenkin's book, *The Cornish Miner*.

John Wesley, the last of my group, was in St. Austell a great many times on his evangelising visits to Cornwall ; he first came into the county in August 1743, but it does not appear that he called at St. Austell on this occasion. But from 1755, when he begins to note in his journal his preaching in the town, up to 1789 when he came for the last time, he must have been with us in all some fourteen or fifteen times. His first notice of us in 1755, when he came over from his friends at Methrose in Luxulyan, is dated Thursday, August 28th : "I preached at St. Mewan. I do not remember ever to have seen the yard in which I stood quite full before, but it would not now contain the congregation ; many were obliged to stand without the gate. At five in the morning I preached at St. Austell to more than our room could contain. In the evening I was at St. Ewe."

And so the record of his relentless energy rolls on through the years to its appointed end ; preaching three and four times a day, always beginning at five in the morning, and riding usually some fifteen or twenty miles.

He was here again two years later, and stayed over Sunday in the town, September 25th, 1757 : " The whole church service was performed by a clergyman above ninety years of age. His name is Stephen Hugo. He has been Vicar of St. Austell between sixty and seventy years. Oh what might a man full of faith and zeal have done for God in such a course of time ! At two I preached in St. Stephen's. . . . About five I preached at St. Austell to an exceeding civil people. But when will they be wounded, that they may be healed ? " Poor parson Hugo, probably a worthy old creature enough ; and he might at least have got a good word from Wesley for the good manners of his parishioners. But no ; that placid and contented way of life had no virtue for Wesley's restless desire to be up and doing. Nor was he pleased with mere politeness on our part ; what Wesley loved, like any other great orator, was to feel that the people were as clay to be moulded in his hands. At Crowan, for instance, in 1765, he is much more satisfied : " I admire the depth of grace in the generality of this people ; so simple, so humble, so teachable, so utterly dead to the world ".

But as the years went on, Wesley found that one of the most steadfast of his societies in Cornwall was that of St. Austell. There had been devoted disciples in the town from the first ; Richard Vercoe had very early held preaching and prayer meetings in his house ; and another pioneer Methodist was Mr. Flamank, of Fore Street, with whom Wesley used to stay, and from whose doorsteps he preached. In September 1769 he was here again : " Mon. 4. About noon I preached in the Lower St., at St. Austell to a very numerous and very serious congregation ; but at Medrose, where was once the liveliest society in Cornwall, I found but a few, and most of those faint and weary." In September 1770 : " Mon. 3. I stood at the head of the street in St. Austell, and enforced on a large and quiet congregation, ' Thou shalt worship the

Lord thy God, and Him only shalt thou serve '." Further visits came in 1773 and 1776 ; on the latter occasion, " the rain drove us into the house at St. Austell, where I think, some of the stout hearted trembled. The next evening I preached at Medrose and was pleased to see an old friend with his wife, his two sons and two daughters."

From 1780 he paid us a visit three years in succession. And then for his last three visits, 1785, 1787, and 1789, his accounts of his stay are much more detailed ; for there are preserved the intimate little diaries into which he jotted his doings almost hour by hour. These diaries, apart from the Journal, are the ultimate proof, if proof is needed, of the amazing activity and tenacity of Wesley's mind ; it is as if he were jealous of every moment of his life that passed. Take the jottings of the day, for example, on Monday, August 22nd 1785 : " On business, prayed, tea ; 4.15 chaise ; 9 Liscard, tea, Acts XVI. 31, chaise ; 2 St. Austell, dinner, conversed, Walsh, letter, prayed ; 6 Gal. VI. 15 ; 7 society, within, supper, prayer ; 9.30 ".

The last journey but one into Cornwall took place in September 1787. On Monday the 10th he writes : " We went on through swiftly improving country to St. Austell, and preached in the new house, though not quite finished, to a crowded audience, who seemed all sensitive that God was there. The old house was well filled at five in the evening, Tuesday the 11th." The " new house ", according to a note in Curnock's edition of the Journal, is now part of the Baptist building in West Hill, and was built on a site given by Mr. Flamank of Fore Street. Wesley's very last visit, in August 1789, was a great triumph and at the same time a little saddening. Everywhere he was received with great honours, and for once in a way he allows the pleasure it gave him to appear ; he must have felt as he wrote that it would be the last time. At Falmouth he wrote : " The last time I was here, above forty years ago, I was taken prisoner by an immense mob, gaping and roaring like lions. But how is the tide turned ! High and low now lined the street, from one end of the town to the other, gaping and staring as if the King were going by. . . ." But the note of sadness creeps in as he records preaching at Gwennap Pit to thousands : " I preached . . . in the evening at the amphitheatre, I suppose for the last time ; for my voice cannot now command the still increasing multitude. It was supposed they were now more than five and twenty thousand. I think it scarce possible that all should hear." And after that, he came no more.

Such are the brief notices which our town and our fore-fathers attracted from the three travellers whose evidence I have chosen to collect. That is how we looked to them, who were after all outsiders, passing about their affairs in the world. But we have reason to be grateful to them, for their notes enable us to catch a precious glimpse of the old place and the old generations ; and so do we defeat Time, the enemy. There is yet another way of recon-structing something of the past ; from the parish registers, old account-books and deeds, and letters. If only one could gather in some place of safety all that remains of this kind from the dust-heaps of the ages, one would have material for constructing a still more valuable picture of our town's past. And so one should conclude with the hope that all who are fortunate enough to possess such memorials of former times will take care to preserve them from the destruction to which too many things of value are consigned by the world. The best way to achieve this is for the town to form a little collection in some convenient common place, where every generation as it passes by may learn something of its forerunners that they may not be forgotten.

TRIBUTE TO A CHINA-CLAY WORKER

SAM JACOBS, as we learned and loved to call him familiarly, died after a short illness of only a few days at his home at Treviscoe on Saturday, June 6th, 1931. When the news of his illness reached me here in Oxford, I could not but believe that he would recover — I had such confidence in that firm unbending frame — and that we should meet yet again to talk over happily the things that we loved to discuss together. And now that will not be ; I can hardly realise that when I come home again and whenever I go out into the clay district, he will not be there to listen, to encourage, and to confide in. Treviscoe will not be the same place without him, I was going to say ; and yet, for me, it never will be without him ; the place is so inseparably associated with his memory.

How well I remember him ; every trait of his outstanding, unmistakable personality is so clearly stamped upon my mind. I see him best sitting upright in his armchair at the head of the table in his own home, listening to the conversation, with the great strong hands that had worked hard and long, folded together, closing and unclosing as we talked ; or joining in with some remark that showed the whole man was behind it, or relapsing again into a friendly silence, following what was being said always with sympathy and keenness, his clear blue eyes lighting up at something that struck some deep chord in him. And so he was at meetings, the most responsive and ardent of listeners ; one always knew, when he was there, that there was somebody whose whole bearing and presence were an encouragement, in whom the entire sincerity of the man would respond. As a speaker, too, there was the whole man, one felt, behind whatever he said ; and that gave, such was his character, a noble quality to what he had in mind to say. I have heard his voice trembling with passion ; but it was always passion for justice, a ringing appeal for what was right, a voice speaking for the poor and downtrodden, for the people who cannot speak for themselves.

He was, I believe, one of the most just men that ever I knew. There was no just cause that had not a friend and a recruit in him. At the same time he was one of the strongest of men. There is no greater or more common mistake than to think that because a man is on the side of what is just and right he is not a strong man. As if the way of sympathy for the weak, of struggling for good causes, were not infinitely more difficult a path than following your own desires, and letting the world go its own way ! For one thing, if you choose the first way, you may have only yourself to depend upon in the end, and in a world where one of the most disappointing and bitter facts is the strength that bad causes can always exert. Such a man, so far from being weak, will almost certainly have to be a fighter for what he believes ; and Sam Jacobs was always such a fighter for the good. There was never any man I knew who combined greater strength with greater tenderness ; surely that perfect balance of character we find most admirable in men ?

It was, however, only in the last two years that I came to know him intimately. But so sterling was his character, that to come into contact with him was to give you the clue to the man. He had a long record of public service ; he was for a time a County Councillor, the first and perhaps the only working man member we have yet had on the Council ; he was a Governor of my old school at St. Austell. In these years he was but a public figure to me ; as a boy at school I used to see him turning in at the gate to attend a Governors' meeting, his keen eye looking over the summer lawns and the well-kept paths ; or, again, I remember an occasional speech at a school gathering. It was only later that I divined all that education meant to him ; I realised then that he had a profound respect, from the bottom of his heart, for education. Such a respect is, perhaps, rarer than we think ; it is more often found amongst men of an older generation now departing. They who fought hard to ensure that a good education, such as they had never had, should be open to all men's children were likely to set a higher value upon what had been won in their lifetime ; it was only natural. It is easier for us, who have not been through that battle, but have enjoyed its fruits, to forget the heat and labour of the day ; and yet, we should not allow ourselves to forget. Only a little imagination should open our eyes to what we owe them.

Perhaps those saw him at his best who saw him in his own chosen movement. To the Labour movement in the clay area, and in the Penryn-Falmouth Division, he stood at the end in the relation of a spiritual father : he was to us all guide, counsellor, and friend. Here, he was not only a good fighter, but a born leader ; one of those men thrown up from time to time by the working people whose instinct it is to lead, whose gift is to strike out independently for their convictions, who will stand firm, freed from convention, regardless of their own interest and whatever any may think.

" Cast thy bread upon the waters, for thou shalt find it after many days " — there was never anything more true said of the essential condition for the leadership of men. Not to be so hampered by immediate circumstances that you cannot see the larger vision of the future ; not to be so confined by narrow considerations of interest that you fail to see the greater things at stake, and perhaps miss the best you are capable of ; the risk involved in these things, the choice between one course and another, is what such a man has to face. But there is always this manifold return of the bread upon the waters ; and at the end of his life, he had in a measure greater than any other, after the earlier risks he had taken, the veneration and the love of hundreds of his fellow men.

Perhaps to him the choice that must have faced him at the beginning, in his leadership of the men in the great Clay Strike of 1913, was less conscious and more natural. I have sometimes wondered how much his gift owed to a soldier's training. For in early life he had been a soldier ; had served in India, and, if I mistake not, had been through one of Roberts' famous marches on campaign. Indeed it was one of my hopes, in writing these impressions, that some day I might take down from his lips the various record of his long life, the reminiscences he might have wished to preserve. But now my hope is in vain, and I am writing this tribute to his memory.

We cannot but grieve for his loss. And yet, in our regret there should be mingled something of pride. He had lived such a noble life ; he had reached, after the years full of event and, I am sure, of happiness, a haven of peace in the fullness of days. And there is this, for consolation. Those who are most lonely and to be pitied at their latter end, I often feel, are those who in earlier days have set their hand to nothing that will outlive them and leave no sign that they have passed this way. There are others who have mistaken, and in youth have set their hand to a cause which has broken and they are left lonely, without posterity, in their last days.

To him this has not happened. He died fortunate in the love of many followers ; he left a living movement as the witness of his life and work. It is of such that the consoling words are written : " The souls of the just shall be had in everlasting remembrance ".

IN THE GYLLYNGDUNE GARDENS

THE other day, as luck would have it, I was to make a speech in the Gyllyngdune Gardens at Falmouth.[1] I had not been in the Gardens, for any time, for a good many years ; and arriving early, I went to find a quiet nook where I might be alone and enjoy the beauty of the place, and, as my habit is, to collect my thoughts before speaking at the meeting.

It was a pleasant little look-out post that I found : a winding alley on the edge of the grotto, with a bench at the end, shaded by the tall trees behind and fringed by low palms, a spot where the bay lies before you, through the greenery of the leaves. Delighted with this cool and charming corner out of the hot sun, I sat down to think over what I should say.

I mustn't forget, I said to myself, to thank the Mayor and the Corporation for their kindness in letting us meet in so lovely a place. . . . I looked round. How beautiful the gardens were ! They were at their best on this June day. The bright sun, that made the lawn and the parterres so gay, that streamed in through the roof of the verandah and lit up the walls with a pale reflected brilliance, shining into the greenhouses and bringing out the colours of the flowers, came only into my nook in little gleams here and there, on the trunk of a tree, a sudden patch of light catching the ivies, or running a sharp line like a sword along the edge of a palm-frond. All was so beautiful that I gave myself up to it ; and the thought of my speech gradually stole out of my head.

I remembered the time when as a child I used to stay at Falmouth in the holidays, and came sometimes to these gardens. How curiously one remembers things from

[1] Written in 1931.

childhood : a few scraps very vividly, unforgettably, and all the rest sunk into the dark background. It is as if everything were strangely out of perspective ; I had forgotten everything out of the gardens, and what they had looked like, except only the tall Australian fern at the bottom of the dark well of the grotto. That was what had made the most lasting impression on my mind ; that and the sea.

There was the sea now at my feet, the long whispering and lapping of the tide running in, just beyond the edge of the garden's greenery. The words of a dead poet came into my mind, to describe the colours of the sea. " The mid-sea blue or shore-sea green " — how exactly he has conveyed, in a phrase, the contrast in the appearance of the sea inshore and out in the bay, just as if he had painted it.

The murmur of the sea was over everything, that soft musical insistence of the sea in summer, that underlay all other sounds and was the burden to them ; an intermittent rise and fall, sometimes the slow break of a wave on the shore the only sound, sometimes passing voices, or a bird singing or the tread of a horse on the road below, rising uppermost above the sea's enchantment. Then, too, there was in the air, lurking in everything, winding itself into the chambers of the senses, the nostalgic smell of the sea.

There is nothing so nostalgic, so characteristic of itself alone, that holds one so subtly to the sense of home, as this sea-smell. I thought of a little note in my pocket-book, written when first returning from away : " This lovely concatenation of scents that tells me I am home again ; escalonia, brushwood, December mould, the sea ".

It goes so to the heart, being home again, I thought ; every cliff and headland, every lane, almost every shore and leaf has more value ; it is as if I am part of it, and it, in some incommunicable way, is bound up with me. How curious it is, I thought, and not a little ironical, that it is not until we go away from it all that it comes to mean so much to us. We begin, when almost too late, to appreciate how rare it is, and how much we owe to it all that we are. And then I wondered, making a last effort against its soft magic, couldn't I bring that into my speech?

But I knew that it was only an excuse, and that I shouldn't make up any speech now. It was happening to me as it happened to the Deputy-Mayor in the story, going to make up his speech in the fields : everything conspired to distract his attention, everything put forth its utmost seductiveness to allure him into a mood of forgetful contemplation. There was a chaffinch hammering away its note in the trees behind ; there were the voices of children in the garden ; a car purred softly over the road beneath ; a wave broke gently, lapsed upon the pebbles and gathered again. Two old ladies appeared in the garden below, and walked to and fro over the shaven lawn, with their attendant gentleman in the wake. A little wind stirred the pine tree on the left, with its bunches of tiny needles, like some submarine plant lost under the waters.

Out in the bay there was one sailing-boat crossing, beautiful as only a bird can be beautiful. Then there came a pair of seagulls crying over the promenade. And I thought of Shelley's sailing-boat and the Bay of Spezzia. Later a little launch came swiftly out of the harbour mouth, rounding the point and with a line of white curving from her prow ; a few minutes and she had blotted the sailing-boat out of view.

I turned to the left, to Pendennis and the cliffs falling away from the Castle hill ; there was the line of the tide at their base, a little way up from the rocks and the sea-weed, and close inshore a white motor-boat riding low and gracefully.

Looking at the buildings grouped together on the headland, with the great stone gateway leading to them, it came into my mind how odd it was that I should know far more about what was going on inside the Castle nearly four hundred years ago than what was happening there today. Indeed, when I thought of it, I knew nothing of its present or what went on inside it now ; and yet of the excitements of its building and furnishing in the days of Henry VIII and Queen Elizabeth, of its early Governors, the Killigrews, father and son, and Sir Nicholas Parker, all of them dead now three hundred years and more, I knew a good deal. Enough, at any rate, to have a clear idea of what sort of men they were when they were alive : a daredevil crew the Killigrews must have been, rather attractive scamps though a sad nuisance to the neighbourhood, with their boarding of ships by night in the river, and their scurrying off into hiding in the country so that nobody could bring them to book. But at last their wild ways and their debts brought them down, and one of the later Johns spent years eating his heart out in the Gatehouse at Westminster. The earlier ones found their graves in the church at Budock.

And I thought of the stirring times they lived in : of that other summer day when the great Armada from Spain went slowly up the Channel, in full view from the Lizard and to the consternation of the watchers on the coast. And again of the time in the late 1590's when a descent was expected on Cornwall, and there were six companies stationed up at Pendennis, one of whose captains was with Raleigh on his first voyage to Guiana, and another on the last ; and of Raleigh himself, fighting against fate, on his fatal last voyage, being driven by head winds into Falmouth for shelter.

My thoughts came to rest at last on that delightful and rare spirit, Caroline Fox, whose life is for me the life of Falmouth in the last century. When I think of her, I

think of some subdued interior scene in the early days
of Queen Victoria : perhaps it is a winter day in the
house at Rosehill and the wintry sun throws a beam upon
the hearth where a bright clear flame is burning ; or
it is a winter's evening, and the curtains are drawn
and in the candlelight the circle of friends are gathered
together ; or again it is a stormy walk amid the showers
and sunshine of February to Pennance and Penrose, perhaps with John and Clara Mill, or with John Sterling,
so brilliant a man and so touching, on whom the hand
of death already lay, yet full of vitality and the love of
life, burning with ideas that he would not have time
to fulfil, inspiring everyone with whom he came into
touch with his own ardent spirit, pouring out from his own
rich stores of thought generously and without stint, his
pale face, with the sensitive lines of nostril and lip, lit up,
his grey eyes ablaze.

Yet they have all gone out of the world ; they have
passed. We all pass : we are but moments in time, I
thought.

So thinking, time passed . . . It must be time for my
meeting ; I must go back to the gardens. I got up from
my seat and, leaving the friendly little arbour of my
retreat, I wondered again, what was it that I had to say
in my speech ?

WEST-COUNTRY JOURNEY [1]

(I)

I WONDER how many of us who have to live away for some part of our time, use quite consciously the image of home that is impressed upon our minds in this way ; who, when they are tired perhaps with the day's work, know how to call up pictures in their mind of what they most love to remember ? All of us, to some extent, do it unconsciously — and so much of our mental life of this kind is only half conscious to us. I find again and again, when bent for long hours over some book — it may be a book of historical documents bearing on Cornwall, or some dull work of learning with little refreshment to the spirit — that a picture of something beautiful in one's memory of home flashes into the inner eye that waits for such consolation. Perhaps it is of some tedious dispute over the possession of a piece of land centuries ago that I am reading, or a vanished name that I pursue through the pages ; and suddenly, to reward me, unexpected, there comes into the mind's eye some picture of the Pentewan Valley in spring, the green hedges starry with primroses, or of the woods coming down to the river there by St. Clement's and going along the leafy lane by Pencalenick, or again the sudden vision of the Helford River that spreads itself before you from the south porch of Mawnan Church. The very names of the places are bells that soothe the tired mind, the spirit starved of home.

I do not speak for myself alone. How many are those, who in a moment of intimacy have told me what dreams of home have nourished them in distant places? " Q." gives, in a charmed word, as a reason for bringing together the poems he has written, that he knows " some of the numbers included have had even the Horatian good fortune to chime in men's hearts through sentry duty in distant lands ". It is not different with the memories of home that we carry always with us ; we may not remember words or their echoes, but these are the chimes that ring in our hearts.

I remember hearing a touching little incident, which those who were telling it may not now remember, but which, when I heard it, I knew I should never forget. There was an old couple who lived in a village by the sea near my home, and as they grew older, all their children left home one by one, as the way is and as needs must, to seek their living in America. And at last the old people went out to them, and made their home there, and were happy to be all together again. Then one Whit-Monday they all went picnicking as in the old days, but down by the lakeside of one of the Great Lakes. The grown-up children were taking the old people out in a boat, quite content and happy. And one of them said, unthinking, as they rowed out : " Isn't it just like being home again ? " But it was too much for the old couple : that memory struck too deep a chord : they broke down into tears. The spring had gone out of the day for them.

And then there was the man I knew, who was a munition-worker in London during the last war. Overworked day in and day out, and too tired for any strenuous breach with routine when the holiday came, on Sundays he used to make his way up from the East End to Paddington to watch the trains come in from the West. He was a Cornishman, and the one thing that refreshed him in homesickness, in all that waste and at such a time, was to hear the soft western speech of his own people that always gives Paddington a certain homeliness to the Westerner.

Such are cases of the instinctive turning of the exile's

thoughts to his home. But it is possible to make it a conscious part of your mental life, to rely upon calling up what you most would remember, when there is the need for some release from the too great oppression of the present, for some refreshment and inner peace. The great strength of being so able to control your mind is that it makes you less dependent upon outside circumstances. It has been said, by Dean Inge I think, that the true sign of the intellectual is that he is never bored ; and it is for this reason, that he who knows how to explore the resources of the mind has illimitable reserves at his disposal, and is less at the mercy of outside circumstances than most people.

(II) WARDOUR CASTLE AND THE ARUNDELLS

Wardour Castle, where the Cornish Arundells still live, was my chief objective in the Salisbury district. But the whole of that fat, rich country round Salisbury is stiff with the peerage : within a few miles on every side there are the great estates, rounded off with woods and plantations, and each one with some great house of historic interest or with old possessions of note and beauty. Wilton, for example, only four miles out on the Exeter Road, is a famous show place with its collection of marbles and pictures ; to me it will be memorable for one of the finest Holbeins I have ever seen, a sombre Tudor portrait of the father of Sir Thomas More, for its courtyard gay with honeysuckles, and for its sweet-toned bells. Not far out also are Longford Castle, where there is another and even better-known Holbein, the portrait of Erasmus ; and Cranborne, where the Salisbury branch of the Cecils have been settled since the time of James I, who granted it to Robert Cecil, the successful rival of Raleigh.

Wardour goes back in the possession of the Arundells

to some two generations before this, to the reign of Henry VIII, when a younger son of the old Sir John Arundell of Lanherne of that time left Cornwall to make his way in the world ; and though he came upon misfortune in the end (like so many people in the sixteenth century) he left enough out of what he had gathered together to found and endow a new branch of the family, and here it has been ever since. The park occupies a splendid position on the crests of a ridge overlooking a little river-valley, through which the main line of the Southern Railway runs from Salisbury to Exeter. And here within the park, as at Sherborne, are two great houses : the Old Castle, now a ruin within its own enclosure planted with cedars, and the splendid eighteenth-century house to which the family later moved.

These two provide a contrast in character and situation that is the making of the park, but is even more revealing of the different character of the times in which they were built. The builders of the Old Castle chose just the site one would expect them to choose for such a house : it stands on a little rise of its own between two higher converging ridges, so that it seems to lie across the neck on guard and command the gully where now the lake is. It is the sort of strong position that the insecurity of the times forced people to choose in the later Middle Ages. Then later, when the necessity of a walled and fortified house had long gone by, and when indeed the Old Castle had been blown up by gunpowder in the Civil Wars (you can see the discolouring of the stones where they were scorched by it even now, though where the walls remain unbroken the stonework looks as good and fresh as if of yesterday instead of four hundred years ago), then when the land had found peace, the family set about building a new house in a more open position, higher up the park, with a wide prospect of the surrounding country. And this in turn was as much in keeping with the character of the later time, the secure age of the Georges, as the Old Castle was of the turbulent days of the Wars of the Roses.

Following my usual plan of going the long way round so as not to miss anything on the way, I went first to Old Wardour. It was a long, tedious, uphill walk in the tepid clamminess of a damp August day, and with the added discomfort of being pursued by a cloud of hungry flies. But the lane was pleasant, narrow, and winding, and quite deserted of traffic; it gave me the feeling of its having not much changed since the days when the old medieval castle flourished, and men rode to and fro, armed and clanking, down this lane. One could almost imagine them, coming over the ridge and down the slopes, emerging like the few harvesters in the maize-green fields, strange shapes out of the steaming mists that enveloped them. Indeed, it was not difficult to think of the first Sir Thomas Arundell, who chose out and fastened upon this spot, coming down this road making for London, intent upon affairs.

He was very much a man of affairs; he had many connections with politics, and it was politics that brought about his downfall. But not before he had accumulated great estates and a fortune. The Reformation in England was the occasion for a gigantic property ramp; the lands of the Church changed hands rapidly, and those courtiers with an astute legal sense, such as it is clear Sir Thomas Arundell possessed, had the chance of making a pretty penny out of it. He was for some years the chief officer of the Court of Augmentations, the office through which the confiscated Church lands were bought and sold; and as such was superbly placed for making a large profit to himself out of its transactions. This he did not fail to do, gathering together a fine collection of properties in Wiltshire and Dorsetshire. I should add that he was a convinced Catholic.

After the death of Henry VIII, whose brother-in-law

he was for a year or two — as long as could be expected
from the matrimonial instabilities of that monarch : Sir
Thomas had married a sister of Katherine Howard —
he attached himself to the party of the Protector Somerset.
Perhaps this was only natural ; Somerset was the head of
another great western family, the Seymours of Berry
Pomeroy in Devon. But when the Protector fell from
power, Arundell, as a prominent supporter of his, fell too.
He was imprisoned in the Tower for a year or more ; and
then in 1552 he was executed, along with the heads of the
Somerset party. With Sir Thomas' head went the estates ;
and only after some time Lady Arundell, more fortunate
than Lady Raleigh in similar circumstances, managed to
get back the core of the property, including Wardour.

In the new Wardour there is a portrait of Sir Thomas,
painted while he was in the Tower ; he is seated at a table,
with his head resting on one hand, while with the other
he is writing away at something — perhaps the poems he
is said to have written while in prison ; he is looking
very pensive indeed, as to be sure he had reason to be.

The glory of the house is its superb great staircase, a
double flight decorated with Adam balustrades, and
leading up under the light of its own cupola to the state-
rooms on the first floor. Here is the dining-room with
the family portraits. I am not sure whether I saw a
picture of that later Sir Thomas Arundell, who went
abroad when a young man to fight under the Emperor
Rudolf on the plains of Hungary to keep the Turks out of
Europe. He won distinction in the battle of the Raab,
and was made a Count of the Holy Roman Empire, but
on returning to England was soundly rated by Elizabeth
for having accepted a foreign title without her permission.
You can read all the correspondence about it and the
poor man's apologies in the State Papers. She refused to
be pacified ; and it was left to James to make it up with
the family by raising it to the peerage. It was in his

reign, too, that the Arundells of Wardour reverted to Catholicism; the elder branch remaining in Cornwall, at Lanherne, had never ceased to be Catholic during the years of persecution.

Catholic families like this were devoted to the monarchy in the time of the Civil War. There is a portrait of the second Lord Arundell, a harsh-looking man with a rough red face and fair bristling hair, whose wife it was that held out in the castle for a week with twenty-five men against the Parliament; and who had the castle blown up a little later rather than have it garrisoned by Ludlow. Then there is a picture of their daughter, who became a nun and lived her life in exile in the English convent at Rouen; there she is kneeling in devotion before a crucifix, the pale face with dark eyes looking touchingly out of the canvas, a curious Counter-Reformation reminder in so English an environment. And opposite there is a large Van Dyck canvas of the Crucifixion, with portraits of the mother and father painted kneeling in one corner; all so typical of the sentiment of seventeenth-century Catholicism, with great storm-clouds hurrying across the landscape, the agonised body dramatic against the background, the figures in an ecstasy of devotion and lamentation. It is so un-English; but then that sort of religious emotion is not at all true to the English character. The story that is told of the picture is that the poor girl so far away, shut up in her convent, wanted to have the picture of her father and mother with her, as a reminder of home; but this not being allowed by the rules, the picture of the Crucifixion was painted for her with their figures in the foreground.

There are portraits, too, of the daughter and heiress of the time of Queen Anne, with whom the Wardour branch came to an end, but who linked up the two branches of the Arundells once more by marrying the Lanherne Arundell of the day. This fortunate marriage came after a brief spell of prosperity under James II, when anybody who was a Catholic was raked out to provide some semblance of a Catholic *milieu* for the advance of his plans. After the Revolution of 1688 there followed a long period of corresponding political nullity. The marriage brought together the old Cornish estates and the inheritance of Sir Thomas in Wiltshire ; and it was on the strength of this that they undertook the building of the magnificent house to which they moved from the shell of the Old Castle, that remains a monument to historic loyalties and forlorn allegiances.

(III) Sherborne and Sir Walter Raleigh

I stopped at Sherborne on my way home, especially because of its connection with Sir Walter Raleigh. Yet there is hardly anything in the town to remind one of that association. The place is full of the memorials of his successors ; but of the strange story of its association with a man of surpassing genius, not a word. However, for one traveller to Sherborne this year, that story, and the thought of how it entered into Raleigh's life, came before everything else.

There is a curious tradition that Raleigh's first acquaintance with Sherborne started with an ominous fall from his horse there ; that he was riding up from Plymouth to London, and that his fall caused him to stop by the roadside a little way out of the town, where now the park is. He must have had many opportunities of admiring the situation of the Castle and its park, and of considering its desirability as a residence, for he was often on that road ; in those days the main road to London from the West passed right under the Castle walls : it has only been deflected in later times. At length, in 1591, when he was at the height of his favour with the Queen, he obtained a grant of it — though not without considerable use of the arts of management. The property belonged to the see of Salisbury ; and Elizabeth made it a condition of the appointment to the bishopric that the grant should be made to her favourite. The Dean of Windsor refused to accept on such terms, but a more compliant person, named Cotton, was found who would, and the grant was made when he became Bishop. Raleigh put the transaction clearly when he wrote to a friend : " I gave the Queen a jewel worth £250 to make the Bishop ".

As long as Raleigh was occupied in improving his position at Court, he cannot have come much to Sherborne. But his good fortune did not last long : he committed the unpardonable error, in the Queen's eyes, of getting married ; and after spending some time in the Tower, he was sent down to Sherborne to cool his heels, and allowed to languish there for some years in exile. While his rivals were getting ahead at Court, Raleigh was thrown back upon the consolations of building and making improvements on the estate.

It was then that he built the house, called the New Castle, the core of which remains and is lived in today ; and he began the plantation of the park around it and the making of the lake between it and the walls of the Old Castle, so that the two now look across at each other over a sheet of water thick with water-lilies, and echoing to the cries of moorhen and wild duck. These were the years, too, of his earlier speculations and ventures, along with his half-brothers, the Gilberts, on voyages of discovery and colonisation. But he kept in touch with politics all the time, and left no stone unturned to reinstate himself in the Queen's favour. He wrote about this time from Sherborne to his friend Lord Cobham : " I want to know how your particular and the general world moves and how the Queen accepted the jewels ; I will not trouble you with the little commonwealth whence I came until we meet. I am preparing for my miserable journey into Cornwall, whence I will hasten towards you." One can see what he felt about being so far away from Court, the source of all power and most delights. He retained his offices as Lord Lieutenant of Cornwall and Lord Warden of the Stannaries, with all the responsibilities and the position they gave him in the West Country.

But one can see also the excitement of those days of danger in the long struggle with Spain, when Spanish ships were constantly in the Channel and upon the western coasts ; and one appreciates the way these men rose to meet it. On August 13th, 1597, Raleigh wrote hastily to Lord Cobham, then at Plymouth, the news he had heard from the Council that " 80 Spanish ships had entered the seas as high as St. Malo's ". He adds, " If you needs will into Cornwall, hasten or you may be sent for. I am yours before all that live." There is a charming postscript by Lady Raleigh, for whom Raleigh had sacrificed so much, saying : " If I could digest that last word of Sir Walter's letter, I would likewise express my love in which I am one with Sir Walter ". The letter is superscribed : " For Her Matt's speciall affairs. To the Right Hon'ble my very good Ld. the Ld. Cobham, Ld. Warden of the Cinck Ports, Her Ma'ts Leiftenant Generall of Kent ; att Plymouthe. From Sherborne, the 13th Day of Aug. at 12 in the night. Hast post, hast hast for life. Post hast, hast post, with spede."

A regular post to the West was instituted a little later, to keep the Government in immediate touch with the outposts of danger, the Channel and Ireland ; for the former posts were laid from Falmouth, for the latter from Padstow ; and thence the stages went, Plymouth, Sherborne, Basingstoke, and Staines Bridge to London.

Raleigh's friendship with Cobham ended in conspiracy and disaster, and with Cobham's laying down his life on the scaffold for the sake of it, to be followed fifteen years later, after long imprisonment and a famous and resplendent tragedy, by Raleigh himself. For the last two years of the Queen's reign Raleigh had recovered his position, and was more brilliant, more arrogant and imperious than ever. Then the crash came with the accession of James, who hated and feared him. Enmeshed in the toils of conspiracy, isolated and distrusted by everybody, Raleigh was forced out of all his employments, tried for his life, and condemned to the Tower. The moment of his fall, there were commissioners down at Sherborne, selling the stock and beginning to cut down the woods ; and the new courtiers flocked round like flies to get hold of the land, as Raleigh had done. Cecil wrote to him that there were many suitors for it, " not so few as a dozen ". Lady Raleigh went to Court and on her knees to James begged that Sherborne might be left them out of the shipwreck of their fortunes. James is said to have said, turning her away : " I maun ha' the land ; I maun ha' it for Carr." Carr, it is not too much to say, was the light of James' eyes.

But it was not so easy to get hold of the estate ; there remained the penetralia of English law to be got through. Raleigh had, for safety's sake, made two deeds of conveyance to his son and heir, with remainder to his brother. By an extraordinary irony of fortune, for it appears to have been purely a clerical error, the essential words of conveyance had been omitted in both deeds ; and for six years the issue lay in doubt while the courts proceeded on their immutable but exasperating way.

Meanwhile Lady Raleigh resided from time to time at Sherborne, her husband a close prisoner in the Tower. She was there twice in 1605, the year of the Gunpowder Plot. And it was noted, for everything the Raleighs did was suspect, that in September of that year " she did cause all the armour to be scoured ". All sorts of dark reasons were alleged, but one person who was examined and who seems to have had a sense of humour, gave it to be, " as he thinketh, because it was rusty ". Again, on another occasion, it was reported that " she caused the house to be dressed up, where before all things lay in disorder ". The truth was that poor Lady Raleigh lived in hopes of her husband's liberation ; hopes which were never fulfilled till too late, when Sir Walter, an old man, was driven on his last, most hopeless and fatal venture, the second voyage to Guiana.

Then, at last, the courts in their own good time and in their own way, pronounced : the flaw in the drafting of the deed was held to invalidate Raleigh's claim on behalf of his son. The King had put up with a long delay, and he was now free to give it to his favourite Carr. Ordinary folk in London, who had never liked Raleigh, commented like the assiduous letter-writer Chamberlain : " So he may say with Job : Naked came I into the world, etc." Raleigh wrote a despairing appeal to the favourite : " I beseech you not to begin your first building upon the ruins of the innocent ". It was all in vain ; Carr knew very well that Raleigh had had no compunction in building upon the ruins of others. The curious thing was that when, after changing hands twice, the King had it in his hands again and pressed it upon Villiers, the succeeding favourite. Villiers, who was a better man than Carr, protested to James, almost as if the echo of Raleigh's words were in his ears : " Do not build my fortune upon another man's ruins ".

So it was granted to Lord Digby, along with the earldom of Bristol, for the strenuous service of having gone twice on embassy to Spain. And in their family it remains.

A good many changes have been made in the lapse of centuries ; the lake has grown, the park and its plantations have been doubled, the old road from the west no longer runs by where Raleigh was first enamoured of the spot. And yet, though there is hardly any memorial left of him there, the whole place speaks of him, for he was the second founder of Sherborne and the creator of the design such as we see it still.

It is altogether so beautiful that, when you see it, you do not wonder at the undying efforts Raleigh made to keep it and hand it down to his son. Yet when you look over the valley with the long ridge of woods and sloping parkland, and across the lake to the walls of the old castle among the cedars and beeches, you know that what Raleigh felt must have been the feeling in the hearts of yet earlier possessors when their day came ; and that Time has defeated them alike and him.

(IV) EXETER — CAPITAL OF THE WEST

I arrived at Exeter late on a beautiful, clear Sunday evening ; too late, alas, to hear the bells of the cathedral that I had been hoping, on the way, to be in time for. For I have always heard of them as one of the loveliest peals of bells in all England ; and I have a passion for church bells. It is perhaps the thing that I miss most subtly in leaving England ; there are all sorts of church bells abroad in their place — the curious chimes in the towers of old German cities, the unlovely nostalgic jangle of the bells ringing out over flat and woodland of the North German plain, the sweet tinkling from little belfries in the Tyrol, the low and exciting boom of the bells from the great Paris churches reminiscent of such dangers and past excitements. But there is something distinctive of England that I miss when out of the range of our church bells : a sweet melancholy, charged with memories, and yet bordering always upon a subdued joy in life.

And this Sunday evening, as I drew near to Exeter in the train, there was a rousing burst of bells ringing to service from the church-tower at Whimple across the cider orchards and blowing in a gust straight into the compartment of the window as the train drew away again from the station.

Exeter is a city that any county, or rather, any country, might be proud of. And yet it may not strike you all at once : you have to put in the sort of apprenticeship I did, wandering around its streets at all hours of the day, keeping your eye open for the old and curious houses that may pop up anywhere, tracing out the lines of the medieval city that subsist unchanged if you follow out the line of streets where formerly the walls went ; and there are all kinds of pleasant surprises you may come upon, here a stretch of the city wall running along behind a row of houses, there a diminutive church that runs into a backyard, or is so cramped by houses on every side that it is forced to take the oddest shape, or again a dark passage that leads to something straight out of the Middle Ages like the Hall of the Vicars-Choral of the Cathedral, or just a ring in the wall where they attached the chains at night to keep people out of the precincts of the Close.

You may be disappointed until you have done all this, and got an inner feeling for the distinctive character that the city has. Coming straight from the green spaciousness of Salisbury Close, with its acres of wide lawns and gardens and the perfection of the houses there, I felt a little apologetic for the Close at Exeter, which is altogether smaller and less beautiful. But the longer I stayed there, the more I saw what a remarkable character of its own the city has, just as remarkable in its way as Salisbury, or Münster, or Bourges.

It may be fanciful, or it may come from dwelling too much upon old times — until in fact I sometimes feel I know what was going on in a place three hundred years ago better than what is happening there today — but the predominant impression of Exeter upon my mind was that of a frontier town. It was unmistakably of the West ;

Sherborne had been an approach to the West, but this was really the key to it. This position has given it its character throughout the ages ; and not all the changes and the indignities that the modern world has brought upon it can altogether overlay the spirit of the place or prevent its genius from appearing. One night, fairly late, I went down the High Street to the bridge across the Exe, and turned back to get a view of the figure the city made. It was like a fortress. At night you could see the bold lines of it standing out as it had always been through the centuries, undistracted by the sights and the disturbing detail of the day. There was the main artery of the city, the long High Street coming bold and straight downhill to where the river was bridgeable ; the bridge carrying the thoroughfare across river and island to the west ; and here at the gate, the danger-point in the city's defences, so often assaulted and so faithfully guarded, the houses on either side crowd together to narrow the entry ; and at night, seeing only the essential lines, I thought how like great bastions they were, with the city wall running up from the river on either side.

Very early on, the Romans made it a frontier town against the unsubdued tribes that we were, haunting the wilds of Dartmoor and the Cornish hills. Then later, in Saxon times, there was in the reign of Athelstan a dual régime in the city, whereby Celts and Saxons lived together in harmony. Even to this day it is noteworthy that on one side of the city you have the Romano-British dedications of the churches remaining — St. Petroc, St. Kirrian, St. Pancras, St. Lawrence ; and on the other side the Saxon saints.

It is the city churches that contribute most to the characteristic appearance of Exeter — or perhaps I should say "lend most", since I gather that some of them are threatened, and certainly it would be a loss to the city's appearance if any of the old ones went. True, there is an extraordinary litter of them, mostly small ones, but that is part of the fascination. Anywhere you are liable to come upon an old church, full of the memorials of past civic greatness, tucked away in a corner, or breaking out of line in the street. They are mostly built of red sandstone, that soft Devon stone which weathers into such fantastic shapes, so that here and there a tower looks as eroded as a rock on the coast.

And inside, though not beautiful, they are so full of character. They are such reminders of the slow tides of a city's life through the ages, tides which seem now to be drawing away from these shores and leaving them high and dry, memorials of a great past. They bring home to one the time when the merchants and tradesmen lived their close, communal life, crowded together in the city, when pride of their own parish and church was strong, and all the little jealousies flourished a while and now are gone. Here they sleep, under the ponderous memorials, beneath the urns, beneath the pews they occupied when alive, the mayors, the burgesses, the aldermen, the successful tradesmen, their little day of local greatness past, themselves the city counterpart of the " rude forefathers of the hamlet ".

Among them, if you look, you will find some Cornish folk who came to this city to make their fortune ; and others who came here to die young, like that Loveday Bellett of Bochym, of whom there is a memorial in the church of St. Pancras. It says, rather touchingly : " She died in this city 16 September 1711, of the small pox, a distemper so remarkably fatal to her family that no less than four of her sisters died of it in the months of February and March, 1716–7 in the boroughs of Penryn and Fowey aforesaid ".

No, I would not have these old worthies disturbed by the Bishop's Commission or what else in the modern age. If it's the traffic, then let them build a by-pass road round Exeter and not destroy what is chiefly lovely in the city.

If it's the lack of congregations, then let them take down such churches as are both redundant and of no attraction anyhow. I have my own solution to offer : it is that if any church in Exeter must go, it should be St. Mary Major, which is of no interest, and standing as it does at the west end of the cathedral is not needed at all ; while its removal would be a blessed improvement to the whole appearance of the Close.

(V) Excursions from Exeter

Exeter is, as the guide-books say, a delightful centre from which to make excursions into the surrounding country. The pleasure is increased by the presence of a convenient new bus centre ; a kind of road station which gives the hardened bus traveller like myself not only a desirable security in the way of catching buses, but, further, even some comfort and shelter while you wait.

However, the real pleasure of making an excursion does not depend upon these material considerations ; it is rather, if I may say so, an affair of the spirit. You have to have some definite objective in mind, to know what you are looking for ; that provides you with the requisite stimulus for getting there, and having got there, a mellow feeling of satisfaction with yourself (if it has been far enough) fills and supports you on the way home. In my excursions out of Exeter I was at least living up to my precept ; for I had come determined to go over the old battle-ground of the Rebellion of 1549.

The ground that was fought over in those far-off days is now quiet enough ; it is all that country, mostly heath and marshland and river-meadow, lying between Honiton and Exeter. The hardest of the fighting was done, and indeed the issue decided, in the area around the river Clyst, a stream that runs athwart the roads leading into

Exeter from the east, and flows down the valley to join the Exe below Topsham.

The Rising in the West is usually called the Prayer-Book Rebellion ; as if it were only a spasmodic outbreak against the introduction of a new form of church service on the part of the benighted Westerners. It was that ; but it was also a great deal more. The new Prayer Book was a symbol to the adherents of the old faith in the West of the encroachments of the new order upon their old beliefs and usages ; and they determined to use the occasion of its being launched for taking up arms on behalf of the old ways. They were conservative ; they were reactionary ; they were a lost cause before they started.

The movement came to a head in 1549, under the mild government of Somerset, and it found leaders of some standing in Humphrey Arundell of Helland, who was the acknowledged captain of the Cornish ranks, and in John Winslade of Tregarrick, and his brother William, who lived at Mithian in St. Agnes : all of them men of property. Sweeping into their ranks various Devon contingents, such as that from Sampford Courtenay where first the Rising broke out, they advanced on Exeter and besieged it for four or five weeks ; and during the summer months of 1549 the Government was for the time paralysed by the struggle.

Lord Russell was sent down to the West and made his headquarters at Honiton against the Cornish camp around Exeter. He had with him a contingent of German mercenaries, trained to formal warfare ; and when reinforcements had made him overwhelmingly superior in force, he advanced along the Honiton-Exeter road. But his passage was fiercely contested ; for a time his army was held up and even beaten into retreat. The advance of the Royal troops was resisted all along the old road crossing the Clyst valley ; Clyst St. Mary itself was set on fire, and by Russell's orders the prisoners taken were killed higher up the valley on Clyst Heath.

As I sat eating my lunch peaceably to myself, in a window looking out on the main street of the village, I could not but think of that other August day, so long ago now all knowledge of it must have perished out of mind among the villagers. And yet here was the same street, and the slope down which the troops came amid the burning houses ; and at the bottom of the hill the bridge and the long raised causeway of red sandstone across the marshes where the Clyst breaks into two branches and spreads itself out over the flats. Here there were bright saffron and purple marsh-flowers to be seen among the weeds and sedge.

Yet another objective of mine while staying in Exeter was the Bradninch country. I had read so often of the Honour of Bradninch, as being parcel of the Duchy of Cornwall, and of the ancient office of Steward of Bradninch, without knowing exactly where it was, that at last I thought I would find out. A strip of high, hilly country, some six or seven miles long and two or three broad, rises up between the valleys of the Exe and the Culm ; that is to say, it lies between Tiverton and Cullompton. This is the Bradninch country ; and a curious and exciting little world of its own it is. For one thing, it is so isolated. The slopes on either side to the valley are so steep, particularly that on the Exe side, up which I toiled in the pouring sun of an August afternoon, that no wonder motorcars avoid it. Besides, there are no first-class roads running through it at all ; and the poor badgered pedestrian, battered as he is from pillar to post on a main road, can take this little world at his ease. That is to say, once he has got up that memorable hill above Bickleigh and is on the plateau.

I had come that day a little disappointed from Tiverton and Sampford Peverell : with the latter because the church was shut and I could not get into it. But my spirits revived with the ardour of having to mount that hill. The Exe valley just here where I struck off the main road is singularly beautiful. Bickleigh Hall, the home of a branch of the Carew family, a fragment of a Tudor house, lies in the valley ; and in the church there are some good Carew monuments, of the seventeenth century mainly ; there is one of Humphrey Carew, who died in 1616, looking faintly ridiculous in full red Jacobean pantaloons and with an inane painted face ; and there are others of the family, connected with Cornwall, a daughter of Sir Reginald Mohun of Boconnoc, and a young woman who married an Erisey and who died young in childbirth.

After looking in at Bickleigh Church, I had no further interruption of my tramp until reaching Cullompton, about six miles across. It was an exceedingly beautiful walk, along narrow and sometimes confusing country roads, where the only danger, in the absence of a map or anybody of whom to ask the way, is in coming to a fork in the road and taking a turning which, one finds after going some way down, leads to a farm-house at the bottom.

This hilly country, I kept thinking, is like nothing so much as the east bank of the river Fowey at home : all those formidable hills from St. Winnow and St. Veep to Lanteglos. But having sweltered and toiled up them, one has such a reward. Here there were glorious views ; back over the valley of the Exe to Haldon and the rim of Dartmoor ; or forward to the Culm valley, and upwards to the Blackdown hills and Exmoor. Moreover, everything is so untouched, unspoiled, in country like this. The road underfoot is stony, because unused by cars ; but then there is meadowsweet growing in clumps in the hedges and filling the air with heavy scent. And there is a superb beech wood you go through half-way across ; the hay-maker who directed me called it a " copse ", but it was as fine a wood of great tall beeches as I have seen for many a day. The trees have had room to grow and they have shot up like pillars in a cathedral, straight and unencumbered, leaving the way beneath cool as in the depth of a well.

I fell in love with this Bradninch country. And if I were asked how and why Bradninch came to be a part of the Duchy of Cornwall, I should be inclined to give a fanciful explanation of it. I should say it was parcel of the Duchy, as was thoroughly right and proper, because by nature it was just a bit of Cornwall dropped into the middle of Devonshire.

(VI) Homeward : the Last Stages

Exeter — Chagford — Okehampton

As I write from a room high up above the roofs of Amsterdam, looking across the steep gables of the old Dutch houses to the steeple of the Oude Kerk, and where even now the chimes of the city are ringing in my ears, I think of the extraordinary contrast of this present that surrounds me and the country of my journey homeward, such a little time ago and now so far away.

This Netherland country has such a character all its own : the green flats spotted by the black-and-white cows and with never a hill, the long straight waterways, fringed with trees, which I had known only from landscapes of the Dutch painters, the luminous expanse of the skies. The last few days I have spent in the dunes between Haarlem and the sea ; a strange little district, where the sand has been mostly planted with trees that are so diminutive, that when you look out of your window you see the odd effect of the houses and villas towering above the surrounding woods. And today in Amsterdam I have been finding my way about this strange town, where the place of the boulevards of other cities is taken by great sheets of water and innumerable canals, where the roads run alongside, neat alleys of red brick with lines of trees now dropping their leaves upon the autumnal waters.

It is attractive ; it has its own beauty, quiet, reflective, like the waters and the pastures. But it is not more beautiful than the way home to the West ; nor has the West any less character than this. The more I see of other kinds of country, the more clearly I see the quality of our own. There is something so secret in it, that it is hard to express ; when I come back first to our moors and downs, I find Stevenson's phrase running in my mind — " home of the silent, vanished races " ; and perhaps that is it. The land seems to hold such hidden memories ; it is so old, the hills are eroded by time ; there is a sharpness, an asperity in the essential lines, and at the same time a certain poignant sweetness : it is that that makes it so affecting to the heart.

But not all my time at Exeter was spent in making pleasant excursions into the country. Before going on with my journey home, I had a patch of work to do in the Library. Not that I object to working in libraries, even on a holiday, when it is so delightful a place to work in as the new City Library at Exeter. It stands at the edge of the Castle grounds, a pleasant modern building of soft-coloured brick dressed with limestone, and is the work of an Exeter man, clearly a good architect. What could be pleasanter than working in such a building, with its long light rooms and cool corridors, and with windows looking on to the green lawns and copper beeches filling the moat of Baldwin de Redvers' castle ? Working there was as pleasant as a picnic.

Besides, such amusing things are apt to happen to one in a library. I was reading there one day, when my neighbour opposite, a youngish man in the thirties, suddenly leaned across and said :

" Excuse me, but do you spell ' desertion ' with an ' i ' or an ' e ' ? "

" With an ' e '," I said solemnly.

And then it struck me how odd it was. He was looking up " desertion " in the *Encyclopædia Britannica*. But whatever for? Was he a soldier who had deserted and was now looking up the penalties? Or perhaps his wife had deserted him and he was trying to find out what he could do about it? Or, on the other hand, was he contemplating deserting her and taking the precaution to look up what he was liable for beforehand? Certainly they were fascinating possibilities for a casual, ordinary-voiced question to raise.

One could linger a long while over a short stay in Exeter. But all good things come to an end, and sometimes they end with something even better. I had no idea how beautiful the upper valley of the Teign is. For some miles from Chagford along the eastern edge of Dartmoor to Steps Bridge, the Teign has cut a deep narrow gorge through the hills, an inland cleft in the moors that reminded me of the heath country of Westphalia. Perhaps it was the bareness of the upper slopes at the Chagford end of the gorge, though I believe these were thickly wooded like the lower end by Steps Bridge until a few years ago. The lower end with its thick oaks and beeches looked more familiar, just like a Cornish river, like the Camel at Dunmere, or the Fowey as it runs through the Glynn valley.

We went in the Exeter bus, climbing these steep slopes and hair-breadth turns in a downpour of rain that lasted the whole evening. It was so heavy that it was quite exciting ; the bus plunged forward like a ship in a world of running water, the panes were covered with sheets of rain, so that the outside world was not very distinguishable, you saw only the trees dripping with water and an occasional glimpse of the river rising very fast and rushing in spate down the gorge beneath, while the bus went forward singing with the rain.

And it rained on and off the whole week-end I was at Chagford. Yet it was not disappointing. There seemed something appropriate to this wild Dartmoor country in these great cloud-bursts, and then a frequent clearing when the colours were wonderful, rain-washed and pure, and the air like wine. And the river was a joy to watch ; it ran through the garden of the old mill-house, which was what the hotel had formerly been. It had risen so high in so many hours ; it filled the whole bed of the stream, rushing, a rich peaty brown laced with foam, with great force in its narrow channel under the granite bridge ; stirring up the fish in the stagnant pools, so that late that evening we could see the young salmon peal coming up-stream to leap the falls.

Chagford, too, is as charming as the gorge. It is an unspoiled moorland village, like Luxulyan or Withiel, with a fine church and with a memory that all Cornish-men should treasure. For it was here that our Cavalier poet, Sidney Godolphin, was killed early in the Civil War. He was an exquisite character, of an extreme sensibility, a frail body but ardent spirit, prepared to undergo all kinds of hardship and to lay down his life for what he held to be right. He fell in a skirmish outside in the moorland ; and the tradition is that he was brought dying into the porch of the house that is now the "Three Crowns" Inn. And well it may be, for it is a house that goes back even earlier than that time ; the bench in the open doorway where he was brought is as old as the house. He was buried in the chancel of Okehampton Church. One can imagine the grief of the household at Godolphin when the news came home to them there.

The road to Okehampton from Chagford skirts the northern edge of Dartmoor, with the breast of some tor always in view. It was, on an autumn morning, singu-larly moving, with the patchwork fields creeping up the sides, encroaching on the wide open spaces, witness to the lasting effort of man in the conquest of nature.

But Okehampton town is unattractive; in a beautiful situation of which it is unworthy. There is a litter of chapels for such as find satisfaction in them, and an arcade of which they are very proud. But the arcade has a notice which gave me some pleasure. It says : " Whereas sundry persons are accustomed to congregate in this Arcade and obstruct the passage way, shout, whistle, play ball or other games, or use indecent language to the annoyance of the owner, occupiers or the public, who wish to do their shopping therein. This is to give notice that the police are empowered to remove any person or persons who are disorderly or offend as above. By Order."

The dogs of Okehampton, which are ubiquitous, combine an unparalleled ugliness with singular ferocity. The moors (I am told) are lovely, but you cannot go on them because of gun-fire. Whether it is the proximity of the military I do not know, but the absence of civilisation I found depressing. The church is a long way off and when you get there not worth seeing. My lying guide-book had said it was one of the finest in Devon. I had intended to stay there a night and go out to see Sampford Courtenay ; but there was no way of getting out there, and now I know why Okehampton is no centre for visitors.

There were two things only to redeem it. One was the Castle of the Courtenays, a little way up the valley from the town ; and the other was a travelling parson in a caravan, who sympathised with my disappointment in Okehampton, and told me what Charles Kingsley had said of it, which was much worse ; he called it " an ugly, dirty and stupid town, with which fallen man by some strange perversity has chosen to defile one of the loveliest sites in the pleasant land of Devon ".

Perhaps this was too strong ; perhaps it has improved

since then ; perhaps Kingsley was laughing up his sleeve. Anyhow I entered it with expectations that were not fulfilled ; I left it with relief.

(VII) The End of the Journey

Okehampton Castle — Tavistock — Callington

Okehampton Castle goes a long way to redeem the town for its lost opportunities ; and it is certainly well worth a visit for its own sake. It stands very finely about half a mile up the valley of the Okement from the town, on a little eminence of its own, overlooked by the higher slopes of the valley and with the great shoulder of northern Dartmoor in full view. The ruins are in a good state of preservation ; most of the walls are still standing and you can follow the lay-out of the buildings and gather the purposes they served when they were occupied so many centuries ago. Here are the guard-rooms and beyond them the chapel, with the outer walls falling steeply to the valley beneath ; on the other side of the court is the dining-hall and the range of kitchens beyond, with the great circular ovens open to the day. These buildings are almost all of one storey, and they form two ranges down the sloping court, converging at the gate-house. I have never had such an intimate feeling with any other castle I have seen ; perhaps it was because this is rather small, as castles go, with its little one-storeyed buildings and pent-houses. But it seemed as if one were very near to the life lived in those roofless rooms, as if it were only yesterday that it was extinguished, instead of in the time of the Tudors.

The castle belonged for three hundred years or more to the Courtenays ; it was one of their chief strongholds in Devon, of which Tiverton, Exeter, Powderham, and Plympton Castles were others, off and on. The buildings as you see them now were chiefly the work of the Courtenays in the time of the Plantagenet Kings. But they were not the founders of the castle ; it was one of the immediate followers of William the Conqueror, Baldwin de Redvers, who selected this spot and made it his head-quarters in this part of Devon. The Courtenays did not come out of France until the second invasion of French-men, in the train of Eleanor of Aquitaine ; and the founder of the family, whose son married Isabella, the Redvers heiress, had for father a natural son of Louis VI, King of France.

Some of the original Norman work of Redvers is to be found in the Keep. This stands high up on its mound, with a flight of stone steps down to the courtyard, and on all other sides a steep fall straight down into the valley. On the day I was there the colours were very clear ; the rim of the moor lapped over the edge of the valley ; there was the sound of gun-fire at intervals and the white clouds going gallantly by in full sail over the high ridge.

Tavistock is clearly one up on Okehampton : a town of clean wide streets and open spaces, and much of its building is in a green stone that gives it a rare appear-ance and character. The last time that I saw a town built mainly of green stone was at Soest in Westphalia, where there are seven churches of green sandstone, like emeralds, lifting themselves above the roofs and the surrounding orchards of the city. That little town has hardly changed within its walls ; it came to a stop with the beginning of the Thirty Years' War, and was left high and dry by it. And now, there is its girdle of walls left, and where the moat used to run outside are orchards.

No doubt Tavistock owes something of its openness to the dukes of Bedford ; at least their grandeur is much in evidence there, as here where I am writing, that district of London where they built in the eighteenth century a series of magnificent squares over their property : Bedford Square, Russell Square, Woburn Place, Tavistock and Torrington Squares, reminiscent of Devonshire and the sources of their wealth and greatness. For the first Russell, who made the family's fortune, founded it upon the property of Tavistock Abbey, the richest monastery in the West, which was granted to him by Henry VIII.

Still, I cannot but think that Tavistock would have been much more interesting if the Russells had left it as they found it; for though an open space in itself is a good thing, it is not so good that a fine abbey church should have been destroyed in order to make one. It wrings the heart of an historian to think that the main road into Cornwall runs right through where the nave of the church was. And there are only a few bits left of the splendour that was destroyed to make a road through it. There is the gate-house; in the churchyard a scrap of cloister; about the premises of the Bedford Hotel a few arched doorways, and what looked to me like the original wall of the monastic garden going down to the river Tavy.

My disappointment was strong enough to drive me on a stage further that evening; and I determined not to stay at Tavistock, as I had intended, but to cross the border into Cornwall and stay the night at Callington. I couldn't have been more fortunate in my choice. I had the vaguest idea of where I was to stay; I only knew that I had never been to Callington before, in all the years I had lived in Cornwall, that there was a church or two I ought to see in the district, and a fine tomb of Lord Willoughby de Broke, who ruled the West for Henry VII.

So I went, on the off-chance; and nothing could have been happier. I was deposited by a kindly bus-conductor on the doorstep of an old-established hotel under a new name (" The Bluecap " late " Goldings ") ; and imagine what a pleasant spur it gave to my feeling of patriotism as a Cornishman, when I found that of all the hotels and inns I had stayed at on my journey, this far surpassed any other.

Everything was right that evening ; all travellers will know the feeling. I even found a friend, after weeks of being alone — someone whom I knew years ago when a child, and who for some reason had kept a kindly place for me in her memory. At dinner we were given an omelette that I ought not to forget, for even in France I have never tasted a better. One can never be above remembering such good luck ; for such happy chances are as important to a good journey as castles and churches and sights. And, when I went out for a stroll before turning in, people said " Good night " to me with such warm and friendly voices, after the way one gets lost in strange towns, that I felt, never more strongly, " this is what it is to be home again ".

CHARLES HENDERSON

I T is hard, very hard, when the news of some great
grief comes suddenly upon one, to abstract oneself in
the very moment of loss, to see again as if at a distance
the friend who was so close, and to help others to see him
for the man he was when he was alive. When he was
alive, I say — and yet I cannot realise that he has gone
from among us. Only last night I came back from the
north to find the dire news awaiting me that Charles
Henderson had died in Rome.[1] I can hardly write ;
yet it is my duty, to his memory (for I think it is what he
would have wished), to those who were dear to him, and
to his friends, to place on record what I knew of him.

He was a person the like of whom we shall not see
again ; his death is an irreparable loss to Cornwall. His
work and reputation were well known throughout the
county ; his name and figure must have been familiar to
numbers in every town and village at home, who had
heard him speak on the history and antiquities of the
county, or had read his articles in the newspapers, or
seen his notes and pamphlets reposing as a guide in the
interiors of our churches. Yet I wonder how many realise
how remarkable his gifts were ; how extraordinary it was
that so much learning, such a memory extending over
a vast field of historical knowledge, should have been
possessed by one who in years was still young. For he
knew by heart not only every hamlet and church in Cornwall, but almost every building of antiquity, every old
farm-house, and, indeed, very often, the fields of the farms
and their names. I think now as I write of a little chal-
lenge he made me one day early on in our acquaintance ;
I was to put to him the name of any farm or old holding

[1] He died September 24th, 1933.

217

in Cornwall (a manuscript list of them had come into my hands and I was checking from that), and he would tell me the parish it was in. He would say when we came to a name like Tregarrick, " There is a Tregarrick in Laneast, and another in ——" — wherever it was ; needless to say he won. But his knowledge was of a very concrete kind ; it rested not only upon books and documents, but upon innumerable tramps all over the country, constant returns to it, ceaseless questionings and observations of all that came under his notice, and very little escaped his trained eye and acute mind. Most of all, what led him on was (I believe) that he loved every hill and valley, every lane and track and field, every rock and stone of the Cornwall that no one knew, or will ever know, as he did.

But all this went along with a knowledge of documents that was no less remarkable. From his school-days, his main hobby had been the searching out, reading, transcribing, and collecting of deeds and documents that threw a light upon the past ; and with the years of adolescence and early manhood this study became his chief passion. What wonder that he was a dozen years in front of any of us that were his age ? When but just from school, he was already known at the Bodleian Library and the Public Record Office, no less than at Exeter and among students at home, as an historical researcher of outstanding gifts. It is told of his viva in the Final Honour School at Oxford, how his examiner turned his questions to actual research among original documents, when it became evident that the candidate knew far more about documents than his examiner, possibly than the whole board of examiners put together. I remember well how intimidating I used to find the speed with which Charles could go through an antiquated legal document, centuries old, in an impossibly difficult handwriting ; but in the end I found it encouraging.

And he was always willing to lay the stores of his

information and experience open to someone like myself, slowly and timidly stumbling along the path he trod with so firm, so masterly, a stride. He was very interested in my researches into the Reformation period in Cornwall, and I was looking forward to his help and guidance when I came to write my book. I used to chaff him and say why didn't he write my book for me, since he knew far more about it than I did ? And I had half promised that I would dedicate my book to him, as the first of Cornish scholars. Alas, the hand that would have guided has been removed ; I can only dedicate my work to his memory.

It was said of Lord Acton, when the great *Cambridge Modern History* was being planned, that if it came to the point, he could have written it all himself from beginning to end without turning a hair. And the same is true of Charles Henderson and the history of Cornwall. Various people have made themselves authorities on different aspects of it ; Miss Mary Coate on the seventeenth century, myself on the sixteenth, Mr. Hamilton Jenkin on the history of Cornish industries — but Charles Henderson alone knew the whole background of it. He was the master of us all.

In his own short life he was prolific of writing. His monographs on *St. Germans Priory* and on *St. Columb Major* were models of what such historical studies should be. His book on *Old Cornish Bridges* I have heard warmly praised by no less an authority than Sir Charles Oman ; and I am glad to remember that it gave him pleasure when I told him of it. In his admirable *Cornish Church Guide*, masterly as it is when you consider all the ground it covers, and indispensable if you want really to know your Cornish churches, he gave to us in Cornwall what I doubt if any other county possesses : a complete guide based on the best and most modern historical scholarship. Then there were innumerable studies from his pen, in addition ; the chapter on our antiquities in the volume of the Preservation Society for Cornwall ; the historical notes on the parishes in Canon Doble's " Lives of the Saints " series. Only a week ago, it is now pitiful to think, I bought the current number of the *Diocesan Magazine* in a Cornish church, at Landulph, because it had what must be his last article : " Notes on Gulval ". Some time, if he had lived, he would have brought together all these various studies and the immense stores of his knowledge not yet drawn upon, into a *magnum opus* on Cornish history. Sometimes he thought of writing a book on Richard, King of the Romans and Earl of Cornwall, at other times on medieval Cornwall ; but at the back of his mind, I am sure, was the idea of writing a standard history of Cornwall from the earliest to the latest times, and it was to this end that his large collections of documents and transcripts were formed. These collections are now the chief monument of his work that remains : and it is much to be hoped that they will be kept together as one collection under his name to commemorate him.

It was not until he came back to Oxford as Fellow of Corpus, some five years ago, that I came to know him ; strange to say, for all that his was a household name at home, I had never met him until he was brought one night as a guest by someone to dine at All Souls. After that he came frequently, and our common interests, our common love for Cornwall, and the things of home, and (I think I may say) our affection for each other, brought us quickly and closely together. I am glad to think that these years of his return to Oxford were the happiest of his life. He did not look back with much pleasure on his school-days ; they were the harsh and difficult days of the last war, and, I suspect, he looked upon school as somewhat of an inter-ruption to his favourite studies. As an undergraduate he was, I gather, shy and diffident of taking much part in the general life of his college. After taking his first class in the Schools, he did not at once return to Oxford, but travelled and lived a good deal in Italy ; and then for a year or two was on the staff of University College, Exeter. But when he had once returned as a don to Oxford, he seemed to blossom out and to develop, to make new discoveries in the world of mind. He ceased to occupy himself so exclusively with antiquarian studies and began to launch out in new directions. If I owe much of my interest in Cornish history to him, I am proud to claim that he derived his introduction to our modern writers, Mrs. Woolf, Lawrence, T. S. Eliot, and Roy Campbell, from me.

His tastes were those of a person of great refinement and cultivation of mind. He had always had a sensitive appreciation of music, which came to him from his mother, as, perhaps, his historical and antiquarian turn of mind came from his father. The two were perfectly combined in him, for even his aesthetic appreciation, as was perhaps right, leaned towards the old rather than to the modern ; he liked above all the music of Bach, Handel, and Mozart, and in painting he admired most the old masters of the Italian schools, of which he had learned much during his stay in Italy.

But it is of his character that a friend should speak ; and it is a rare honour in life to enjoy the friendship of such a noble character as his was. He possessed that quality that is the most attractive thing in a man, the combination of strength with gentleness and restraint, of great gifts with simplicity of heart. I never knew him to speak or think ill of anyone ; his was one of the most pure and good natures that I have ever known. He had a shy and whimsical sense of humour, which he could use very effectively to defend himself upon occasion, or to turn the point of an outburst from some more impatient spirit than his own, up in arms against some foolery of the world or some absurdity of opinion. Indeed, he had a very wise tolerance of all sorts of opinion he did not agree with ;

perhaps because he was not vitally concerned in their conflict, and where the most cherished interests of his mind reposed, in the realm of values, he had the gifts of discernment, much joy and certainty of conviction. Much happiness, too, came to him by his marriage, and through the wide circle of friends that gathered round him ; it is some consolation to think that when death came, it came not in defeat, nor in loneliness, but in the flood-tide of good fortune and happy success. It may be some consolation to his parents and to his young wife, to whom the sympathy of all Cornwall will go out, that we are proud to claim in him, for all his youth, one of the most gifted and distinguished Cornishmen there have ever been.

In the end, I think of him now as I used to see him, stretching out his long length in the blue chair in my room at All Souls, or looking out of the window in his own rooms at Corpus upon that tranquil walled garden and its trees, or striding through the shrubbery at his beloved Penmount, or halting in the churchyard at Kenwyn on our way to Lis Escop (that churchyard which he thought the most beautiful in Cornwall), to look back at Penmount among the trees on the crest. Now he lies far away from home, in the eternal city, where lie those other two young Englishmen, Shelley and Keats, of whom the one wrote of the other (I recall the majestic words as a solace in our grief) :

And he is gathered to the Kings of thought
Who waged contention with their time's decay,
And of the past are all that cannot pass away.

THE END

Printed in Great Britain by R. & R. Clark, Limited, *Edinburgh*